The
Life of Quong Tart

Or,

How a Foreigner Succeeded in a
British Community

Compiled and Edited by

Mrs Quong Tart

SYDNEY UNIVERSITY PRESS

SYDNEY UNIVERSITY PRESS
SETIS at the University of Sydney Library
University of Sydney
www.sup.usyd.edu.au

Originally published in Sydney by W. M. Maclardy in 1911.

The publication of this book is part of the University of Sydney Library's
Australian Studies electronic texts initiative. Further details are available at
www.sup.usyd.edu.au/oztexts/

© 2004 Sydney University Press

ISBN 1 920897 80 1

For current information see http://purl.library.usyd.edu.au/sup/1920897801

Contents.

Introduction.

Author's Notes.

This book contains the biography of the late Quong Tart, and was begun on the seventh anniversary of his death. For two years before I married Quong Tart, I kept many of the newspaper cuttings referring to him, and after marriage continued to do so. Sometime in the year 1900 I showed him a bundle of clippings. He said: "Very good; keep them safely; some day I shall have them put into book form to hand down to the children and let them see, although their father was a Chinese, he could be creditably compared with thousands of European fathers." The opportunity to carry out that idea did not present itself till this month, when I found I had leisure, for, at the time of my husband's death, I was left with six children, whose ages ranged from sixteen years to three months, so that my time was fully occupied in giving them a mother's sole care, and striving to bring them up to be a credit to their father's name, for Quong Tart had won from all classes, by his natural and genuine kindness, a character and name impossible to be bought for money; in fact, he so endeared himself to rich and poor alike, that his name became a household word, for, as the "Daily Telegraph" of October 10th, 1897, said: "Quong Tart is as well known as the Governor himself, and is quite as popular among all classes," and this remark, I think, will be fully verified by the perusal of the following volume.

MARGARET TART.

"Gallop House,"
  Ashfield, July 26th, 1910.

The Life of Quong Tart.

or, How A Foreigner Succeeded In A British Community.

Quong Tart was born in the Canton district in 1850, and was the second son of his father, who carried on the business of an ornamental wares merchant for many years in that part.

At a precociously early age, Quong Tart began to make enquiries about those lands which were to be found in the "centre of the earth." The superstitious belief that every Englishman was red-headed, and that as a race the Britishers were a terribly ferocious, man-eating and boy-murdering lot, instead of filling Quong with overwhelming fear, served to whet his curiosity. He resolved to see the outer world, but there was the difficulty, how was he to get away from home? At last there came to his quiet home, tidings of the fabulous wealth which could be collected on the Australian goldfields. Quong was only nine years old, but such was the earnestness of his pleading that he obtained permission to accompany an uncle of his, who was journeying to the sunny south. His uncle was going to Australia to take charge of a lot of Chinese, and it was intended that little Quong should act as interpreter. However, little Quong had made up his mind to try his luck on the goldfields, and decided that the interpretation could be relegated to any who might choose to do it.

He arrived in New South Wales, where he was favoured by the fates in having as his guardians the well-known families of Messrs. Simpson, Want and Scarvell. In 1859, Mr. Percy Simpson, brother of the distinguished Supreme Court Judge of that name, who is now Sir G. B. Simpson, leased the great alluvial area on the Braidwood goldfields known as Bell's Paddock, where he employed many hundred miners, principally Chinese. Mr. Tart, who was then about nine years old, rode a very small pony, and accompanied Mr. Simpson among the miners as an embryo interpreter.

He went to the goldfields, expecting to find the precious metal in great lumps, and he thought that the only thing required to be done was to rake it together and "realise." But how different the anticipation and the realisation! Instead of it being all gold and no work, it was all work and very little gold. Soon after he landed little Quong's bravery sustained a severe shock. He had always ridiculed the tales about the people in these climes being man-eaters, until one day he saw a brutal-looking fellow take deliberate aim with a gun at what Quong thought was a boy in a tree. The man was a good shot, and down came the "boy," and away went Quong as fast as his nimble legs would carry him. He thought that he had at last seen a veritable man eater, who, wanting a delicacy for his dinner, had shot a boy. Quong, then as ever, was anxious to see wrong righted, and his alarm about the man-eating murderer led to enquiries and the disclosure of the truth. What was shot was a "'possum up a gum tree."

He was educated by Mrs. Simpson, who took a lively interest in his welfare during the years he remained on the field, and, on leaving, Mr. Simpson gave him a big interest in an important gold claim, which the fortunate young protege turned to the best advantage. Mr. Tart employed about two hundred Chinese and Europeans, and in the course of a few years his mining speculations made him a comparatively wealthy man. He built a beautiful villa residence at Bell's Creek, erected a school and a church at his own expense for the benefit of the European miners and their families, and was soon after gazetted a member of the School Board. Mr. Tart became a patron of cricket, horse-racing, and every manly sport, and was in truth the most notable resident on the Braidwood goldfields, to whom many families were indebted for assistance, employment and other advantages. Mr. Tart was associated with many Scotch families on the diggings, from whom he acquired a good knowledge of the Caledonian customs, manners and habits. He could sing Scotch songs with singular pathos, recite Burns' poems with a genuine accent, play Scotch airs on the piano, and jokingly alluded to himself as being a native of Aberdeen. He governed to a large extent the Chinese settled on the surrounding goldfields, adjusted their disputes, gave those needing it employment, and minimised all Chinese difficulties.

A certificate of naturalisation was granted to him on the 12th July, 1871, and he was Government Interpreter for the districts of Braidwood, Araluen and Major's Creek, and he was elected a member of the Manchester Unity Lodge, No. 46, on the 31st of August of the same year. He was the first Chinaman elected to an Oddfellows' Lodge in New South Wales. Afterwards he also became a Forester and a Freemason.

In 1874 Mr. Tart had reached the zenith of his popularity on the goldfields; he was then a young man filled with energy and vivacity, in well-to-do circumstances, and it is more than probable that had he offered himself for Parliamentary honours at this period he would have been returned as member for the Braidwood electorate. He did not, however, aspire to such distinction; but resolved on leaving the district to try his fortune in some other speculation. As soon as Mr. Tart's intention was made known, the residents, including all classes and creeds, decided on entertaining him at a public banquent at the Commercial Hotel, Braidwood, where at least two hundred gentlemen assembled. Judge M'Farland took the chair, and the toasts were proposed by Mr. Solicitor Scarvell, Messrs. Maddrell, Bunn, Hassall, and Roberts, Js.P., who spoke of their distinguished guest in the highest terms of appreciation, to whom they presented an address and valuable souvenirs in gold and silver, as a practical testimony of the citizens' esteem. Mr. Tart replied in a felicitous and manly speech, and concluded by singing "Auld Lang Syne."

On reaching Sydney, Mr. Tart matured his plans to establish himself in the metropolis as a tea and silk merchant, and this necessitated a visit to China to perfect his arrangements in that quarter. When leaving, he received letters and credentials from the Premier and principal residents, and in due course reached the home of his progenitors. Mr. Tart visited Hong Kong, Canton, Nankin, and many cities in the southern portion of the vast Empire, where, on introducing his credentials, he was received with high marks of favour by the principal Officers of State, to whom he related the satisfactory condition of Chinese subjects in British territory, where they had the utmost freedom and protection, and discussed the opium question, which he regarded as having a demoralising effect on many of his countrymen. He was assured that the Chinese Government, notwithstanding the difficulties arising through the customs and international law, would do everything possible to minimise the evil.

Crowds followed Mr. Tart as he moved from place to place. Strange remarks were sometimes levelled at him, but they were always received in good humour.

He was entertained by several distinguished Mandarins, who made suitable presents, and introduced several Chinese ladies at their special request. Mr. Tart's sojourn in his native land was not, however, without incident. He visited a village in the Province of Foo Chow, the great centre of scientific agriculture, where the inhabitants regarded him as a rare curiosity, owing, probably, to his being dressed as an English gentleman, and wearing a black silk hat. While inspecting some ploughing operations in an adjacent field, a buffalo attached to the plough took fright, bolted, smashed the plough, rushed frantically through a narrow street in the village, upset the street stalls and their occupants, and did much damage to property. This incident caused indescribable excitement, not only amongst those concerned, but also the entire residents, which was, after a brief period, allayed by Mr. Tart paying three-fold for the damaged property. So pleased were the citizens at the stranger's liberality that some of them were most anxious that he should inspect other field operations, but Mr. Tart declined with thanks, on the ground that he had gained sufficient experience in that line.

During his visit his mother was most anxious that her son should get married, for, unlike most of the well-born Chinese, Quong Tart had no one selected for him when young, and she herself selected several Chinese women of distinction, who would willingly have accepted him. But, again, Quong's good sense asserted itself, for he told his mother that when he did marry, it would be a European, for a Chinese woman in Australia would be but little help for him in carrying out the good works he intended doing.

On returning to Sydney, Mr. Tart not only established himself as a tea and silk merchant, but also opened various restaurants in the arcades between George, King and Pitt Streets, on a scale of splendour never before seen in Australia; and it was here that for years Mr. Tart on various occasions, entertained in a princely fashion, free of charge, large numbers of clergymen and representative gentlemen visiting Sydney on synods and conferences, and acted most liberally in all matters affecting the social well-being of the poorer classes of Sydney, regardless of creed or country. This was exemplified in a special manner, when he inaugurated the movement to provide annual treats for the inmates of the Government institutions in Sydney and the County of Cumberland. He obtained the patronage of Lord and Lady Carrington, and the cordial support of Chief Justice Darley, the Supreme Court Judges, Minister of the Crown, the heads of the various religious denominations, and many influential citizens.

Mr. Tart's labour on behalf of the poor was in keeping with his generous nature. He acted on the principle of the Quaker, who wrote: "I expect to pass through the world but once; if, therefore, there can be any kindness I can show, or any good things I can do, to any fellow human being, let me do it now, for I shall not pass this way again."

In 1883 numerous disorderly proceedings took place at several Chinese camps, principally in the Riverina portion of the colony, during the shearing season, which members of Parliament denounced in scathing terms. Inspector-General Fosbery took prompt action to have the causes of these disturbances thoroughly investigated, and, with that end in view, recommended to the Premier (Sir Alexander Stuart) the appointment of Mr. Brennan, the then Superintendent of Police, and Mr. Quong Tart as a commission of inquiry, which was approved, and the reports furnished by those gentlemen at the termination of their investigations covering the conditions of Chinese camp living, justified in a special manner the wisdom of their appointment. Mr. Tart's reminiscences of that tour would form a volume of interesting reading.

In addition to the able reports on the Chinese camps, for which he was thanked by the Government, Mr. Tart published an interesting pamphlet, designated "A Plea for the Abolition of the Importation of Opium," which had a large sale, the proceeds of which he applied in aid of the Bulli Disaster Relief Fund. Large meetings were held in Sydney by ladies and gentlemen favourable to the views propounded by Mr. Tart in his pamphlet, when resolutions were unanimously carried, and embodied in a petition to the colonial Legislature, praying for the passing of drastic measures in the matter of opium importation. Mr. Tart furnished the principal officers of State in China with copies of his report on the Chinese camps, his pamphlet against the importation of opium, and other proceedings relating thereto, and in due course these were acknowledged with thanks.

In 1886 he married Miss Margaret Scarlett, of Liverpool, England, and was very happy in his married life, and his children (of whom there are six, two boys and four girls) combine all the cleverness and good qualities of their parents.

In 1887, as a result of the first visit to Australia of two Chinese commissioners, he had the honour of a Fifth-class Mandarin conferred upon him for valuable services rendered on behalf of his countrymen, and three years later he was further honoured by being advanced to a Mandarin of the Fourth-class, combined with the extra degree of the peacock's feather, a distinction equivalent to a K.C.M.G.

Chinese distinctions, unlike those of Europeans, travel backward, and not forward; that is to say, they are not hereditary. The Chinese idea, which may or may not be superior to our own, is that if a living personage is worthy of distinction, such honour should not descend to succeeding generations, but be fastened upon his forefathers.

In 1888, during the Chinese difficulty, he was appointed a mediator, and when he paid another visit to his people the following year, for his services in that respect, the Viceroy sent a special steamer to convey him up the river, and he was received with a guard of honour — a distinction never conferred upon anyone else, with the exception of Imperial personages.

At every port of call on his way home, Mr. Tart was received and honoured by leading public men, including Sir Thomas M'Ilwraith (Brisbane) and the Hon. John Douglas (Thursday Island). At Hongkong the leading merchants, including Dr. Ho Koi, a member of the present Upper House, received him handsomely, and he was able to explain to them the actual state of public feeling in Australia against the admission of the Chinese, which had the effect of softening considerably the bitterness entertained towards the people of this country.

On August 19th, 1902, a murderous attack was made on Mr. Tart at his business place in Queen Victoria Markets, and although it did not immediately prove fatal, it was really the beginning of the end, which occurred on July 26th, 1903.

He had been 44 years in Australia when pleurisy took him off at the age of fifty-three, leaving a wife and six little children to mourn the loss of a true husband and a loving father. He was one of "nature's gentlemen," and no man in the city of Sydney was more widely known or respected, and indeed it will be long before we look upon his like again. Quong tried hard to encourage all kinds of sport, and one of the proudest days of his life was that on which he was asked to act as starter and fire the pistol at some pedestrian sports in Sydney. No social gathering was considered complete unless Quong was there to whoop up the praise of "Annie Laurie," and I really believe very little persuasion would have induced him to don the kilts and dance the "Gillie Callum."

In conclusion, I can only say Mr. Tart's life was a series of good deeds, and whose aspirations tended to the realisation, of the noble sentiment —

> When man to man o'er a' the world
> Shall brothers be for a' that.

Marriage.

Quong Tart was married in 1886 at the residence of the late Hon. J. H. Want, Darlinghurst. The late Dr. Steel performed the ceremony in the presence of twenty friends, many of whom have since joined the Great Majority. The honeymoon was spent in Ballarat, Victoria.

"Mr. and Mrs. Tart were met at Melbourne and escorted to the Spencer Street Station by Messrs. D. Ham, M.L.C., J. Oddie, D. M. Davies, A. Young, and J. Russell, M.L.A. At Geelong Station a large number of the leading citizens were assembled to meet the newly married couple. Hearty cheers were given by the Geelong people as the train steamed away from the station, and when it arrived at Ballarat East there were fully three hundred persons — the ladies, of course, predominating — assembled to witness the arrival of the Chinese merchant and his wife, and when the train drew up, the carriage occupied by Mr. and Mrs. Tart and a couple of friends was rushed by quite a hundred persons eager to see them. As the party alighted three cheers were given, and Mr. Tart shook hands heartily with those to whom he was introduced by ex-Mayor Scott; in turn he introduced Mrs. Tart to the various Town Councillors, who had assembled to do him and his wife honour."

Seven of the busiest days of their lives were spent at that time, visiting institutions, attending banquets and entertainments of every character. An instance of one day's programme — "Mr. and Mrs. Tart visited the various institutions in the district yesterday. They were accompanied by Mr. W. Scott, J.P., Miss Scott, Mr. J. Ferguson, J.P., and Mrs. Ferguson. The first place called at was the Benevolent Asylum, where the party were received by Mr. Joseph Phillips, the President, and Mr. Oddie, J.P., Member of Committee. Mr. Tart, who made a thorough inspection of the institution, asked a number of questions regarding the mode of management. Before leaving he said the Asylum was a credit to Ballarat, and as he took considerable interest in kindred institutions in New South Wales, he would endeavour to turn his visit to good account upon his return to Sydney."

When going through the house, a number of Chinese inmates, upon being told who the visitor was, rushed forward, and clasping Mr. Quong Tart's hands exclaimed, "Him welly fine gentleman; him welly good gentleman." Mr. Tart conversed with the Chinese in their native language.

The next place of call was the Hospital, where Mr. Alexander Hunter, J.P., was in waiting to receive the visitors. Mr. and Mrs. Quong Tart and the other members of the party spent some time here, visiting all the wards, Mr. Tart shaking hands with the patients lying in the various beds, and making enquiries as to their state of health.

The Sydney merchant and friends next started for the Orphan Asylum in Ballarat East. Quite a display was here made in honour of Mr. and Mrs. Quong Tart. The boys paraded on the "square" like soldiers, and, headed by their band, stood to attention as the party approached. Then the band played "For He's a Jolly Good Fellow." Mr. Tart then addressed the boys, expressing pleasure at their healthy appearance, and at the tidiness which was shown in their attire. He then presented Mr. and Mrs. Kenny, on behalf of the orphans, with lollies. Cheers were given for the donor as he left the yard, the band playing "Auld Lang Syne."

The Female House and the Water Commission Offices were next visited in turn.

At night Mr. and Mrs. Tart were entertained by Mr. and Mrs. Gale.

"Mr. Quong Tart and his wife were entertained at a banquet at the Eastern Town Hall by a number of leading citizens. The Council Chambers were nicely decorated for the occasion and every provision had been made for the comfort of those in attendance. During the banquet the Ballarat East Band played a number of lively airs in Barkley Street in honour of Mr. and Mrs. Tart, and subsequently the band serenaded the newly-married couple. The loyal toasts were drunk with enthusiasm; Mr. Quong Tart, who glories in being a naturalised British subject, calling for three cheers for the Queen and Royal family. The Mayor next proposed, amidst applause, 'Our Guests.' In so doing, he formally, on behalf of the residents, welcomed Mr. Quong Tart and his bride to Ballarat. A number of other toasts were proposed and honoured. During the evening, Mr. Scott, J.P., on behalf of her husband's intimate Ballarat friends, presented Mrs. Quong Tart with an elaborate Colonial gold bracelet, with a tiny padlock fastener, which bore the following inscription — "Presented to Mrs. Quong Tart, Ballarat, 3rd September, 1886." Mr. Quong Tart returned thanks in a feeling manner on behalf of his wife. A poem in honour of Mr. Tart's wedding, and composed by a resident of Ballarat, was read during the evening as follows:–

Welcome and Good-Bye

No strangers here — but brothers all;
In harmony each loving heart
Bids welcome in this festive hall,
    At Friendship's call
      To thee, Quong Tart.

May peace and love surround thy life,
And never from thy home depart;
May God Keep far from thee all strife;
Preserve and bless thy loving wife
      And thee, Quong Tart.

And as we welcome thee this day
With loving and with open heart
So will we speed thee on thy way —
    Long live Quong Tart!

"The proceedings were enlivened by vocal and instrumental selections and at the close of a most enjoyable evening wedding cake was distributed amongst the assemblage.

"Each day of their stay in Ballarat Mr. and Mrs. Quong Tart were the recipients of public and private hospitality."

Clipping from the "Sydney Bulletin," 18th September, 1886:– "It is said that since the marriage of the happy Quong Tart the visits of the quondum lady customers have become comparatively angelic, or few and far between. This doesn't surprise us in the least. We have always declared the dear girls used to go not for their tea, but their nice little Tart, and now he is married! Yum, yum."

Among the wedding presents, which were numerous and costly, were the autographed photos of Lord and Lady Carrington — four feet by two feet — which were sent with the following letter:–

22nd September, 1886.

Dear Mr. Quong Tart, —

I am directed by His Excellency and Lady Carrington to forward you the enclosed likenesses of themselves as a slight souvenir, and hope that you will accept them and approve of them.

Wishing you every happiness in your married life,

I am,
Yours very truly,
E.W. WALLINGTON, P. S.

JAMES ODDIE., J.P., of Ballarat,
and His Guests, Mr. & Mrs. QUONG TART, of Sydney.
(Who were on their Bridal Tour).

By "Silverpen."

When I heard that Mr. and Mrs. Quong Tart, of Sydney, were to be entertained by the above-named gentleman, I felt sure a most enjoyable time would be the outcome.

By ten o'clock, a carriage and pair of greys drew up before ex-Mayor Scott's residence, Victoria Street, awaiting, the guests of the day, who were driven to the Grand Studio of Mr. Chuck, Sturt Street. The artist secured several splendid negatives of the bride and bridegroom, together with Mr. and Miss Oddie.

The party then visited Lake Wendouree and the nursery of Mr. George Smith; Mr. and Mrs. Tart expressed themselves highly delighted with all they had seen.

At two o'clock, Craig's Hotel was the meeting-place of the invited guests, numbering about twenty, who sat down to a splendid spread. Amongst those present we might name — Rev. J. W. and Mrs. Inglis, Hon. D. Ham and Mrs. Ham, Mr. D. M. Davies, M.P., and Mrs. Davies, Mr. Young, M.P., and Mrs. Young, Mr. Wm. Scott, J.P., ex-Mayor of the Town and Mrs. Scott, Mr. George Smith, Mr. Henry Glenny, J.P., Mr. J. Ferguson, J.P., Mr. J. Robson, Manager of Mercantile Bank, Miss Oddie, and the special guests, Mr. and Mrs. Quong Tart.

Mr. Oddie excelled himself as toast-master, host, and speechmaker — his little impromptu speeches were in every way practical and quite in keeping with the occasion, and of such an enthusiastic and intellectual kind as kept the company in the best of humour.

Mr. John Robson, as leader of the Liedertafel, sang a charming song, accompanying himself on the piano.

Messrs. Ham, Davies, and Young responded for the Legislature — Upper and Lower House. Mr. George Smith, in proposing the toast, declined to say whether or not he approved of their "goings on" down there, and amusingly referred to the strange fact of meeting no less than twenty members of the House at one time visiting the Japanese Village during the session.

Mr. Davies, M.P., responding (amidst much laughter), said the incident could easily be accounted for, inasmuch as it was on the evening of Mr. Harper's diatribe on Theology, and the infliction was **too** much for the **"noble twenty,"** so they, to escape, were glad to flee to **Japan** or any other place. He (Mr. Davies) was not one of the escapees, as he "sat it out" to the last.

Mr. John Robson took the dual part of proposing "The Ladies," and responding — the fact of having to respond to the toast he proposed caused uproarious laughter. Mr. Robson, however, acted well his part.

The Rev. J. W. Inglis, Presbyterian Minister, in responding to the toast of "The Clergy," spoke as usual in a "hit-him-all-round" manner, not forgetting the "only bachelor" present, who received several hints as to his loneliness, the reverend gentleman offering to do the business by special license without fee or reward. In closing his neat impromptu speech, the speaker referred to the uniform kindness of Mr. Tart to Ballaratarians visiting Sydney.

Mr. H. Glenny, J.P., responded for the press, believing that the press was the great educational lever of the world, and feeling assured that Ballarat people need not, wherever they go, be ashamed of their local newspapers, represented as they were by "The Star," "The Courier," and the "Evening Post."

Mr. Tart, in responding to the toast of "Our Guests," made several good hits, and caused much amusement by his native wit. He thanked Mr. Oddie heartily on his own and Mrs. Tart's behalf for his great kindness, and said he had received so much kindness since he had been in Ballarat that he should always have a warm place in his heart for both the place and its people.

The singing by the company of "God Save the Queen" ended this part of the day's programme.

Band and Albion Mine.

After dinner carriages were in attendance to convey Mr. Oddie's guests to the Band and Albion mine. Mr. Waters, the underground manager, met the party there, and kindly took them over the works. The ladies were quite delighted with Mr. Oddie's lucid explanations of the way the gold is extracted from the quartz. The battery was set "a-going," and somewhat astonished Mrs. Tart and the other ladies as the stampers pounded away at the golden stone. Every part of the machinery shed was visited, the Chilian mills and pyrities furnace not excepted. Mr. Waters washed out about £20 worth of amalgam, and allowed the ladies to handle the golden ball.

The Observatory.

The observatory, Mount Pleasant, was the next and last visit made; here the party were met by Mr. and Mrs. Baker and family, who were most kind.

It was incidentally mentioned that Miss Baker, who presided over the impromptu tea so pleasurably, was the first lady in Victoria who passed the Matriculation Examination.

Mr. Oddie, at the Observatory, was in his best form, as the place owes its existence to his love of science and his liberality. No wonder the little ones in East and West Ballarat call the place "Oddie's Observatory." Mr. Baker, the Ballarat Astronomer Royal, took seemingly great delight in showing the party every item of interest in his little "Star Bottling Castle."

A small steam engine was at work, its action being brought to bear all over the workshop.

The big telescope and its mysteries were viewed with wonder. All wishing that we could but have a peep at the starry firmament, through the aperture in the roof.

Mr. Baker is now busy at work at a much more powerful instrument, so that in the days to come, when the "good James Oddie" has passed away, our little ones will be taught to speak of him as the "Young People's Friend," who devoted his time and money unsparingly to advance the best interests of the citizens of Ballarat, where he will ever be known as an honoured citizen and a Christian gentleman.

A visit to the Jubilee Singers by some of the party, and a dinner given in honour of Mr. and Mrs. Quong Tart at the residence of Mr. and Mrs. Ferguson wound up one of the most pleasant days spent in the colony, and one not likely to be forgotten by the special guests of the day, Mr. and Mrs. Quong Tart, of Sydney.

Four Horse Drag and Outriders.

It is as well perhaps to say that Mr. Oddie intended, if the day proved favourable, to take his guests out to Learmonth, and for that purpose had arranged for a four-horse drag and outriders, so that, had this been carried out, the crowd of sight-seers, who surrounded the carriages at Craig's, and cheered the bride and bridegroom before the party left for the Band and Albion, might have had the novel sight of mounted postillions, one not often seen in Ballarat. The clerk of the weather, however prevented the programme being carried out by Mr. Oddie in its entirety.

During their stay in Ballarat Mr. and Mrs. Quong Tart visited the Gong Gong, accompanied by Mrs. and Miss Scott, Mr. H. and Mrs. Glenny, and others, Mr. and Mrs. Minogue, the Reserve-keepers, showing the party every hospitality.

Mr. and Mrs. Tart's visit to Ballarat on their wedding tour will long be remembered.

Quong Tart — Business Man.

Mr. Tart was singularly endowed with great business capacity. Very few men could engineer success in the business line better than he could. Sagacity, forethought and the courage to act swiftly and unerringly in the carrying out of his schemes, traits of character which mark the really successful merchant, were developed in him to an unusually large degree. To perceive an opportunity is good, to seize it is better, to make the most of it when it is in one's possession is best. Quong Tart's ability for making opportune seasons yield their utmost was remarkable. Yet in all his dealings with men he had a strict regard for justice, and its principles were never sacrificed in the quest for gain. He thought it better far for a man to fail, than found a business on unjust principles, and build it up on the broken lives and bleeding hearts of men. In all his business relations he wore the white flower of a blameless life. Said Sir John Robertson, "Quong Tart was no ordinary man. He attained a high position in the city of industry, integrity and energy, and that in the face of the fact that he came of a race not held in favour by the people." The story of his rise from obscurity to publicity, of the difficulties he surmounted on the way, and the manner in which he came to be recognised as one of Sydney's leading merchants and citizens, reads like the wonderful tales of "Aladdin" or the stories of the "Arabian Nights."

A lad of nine years of age when he landed in New South Wales, he was sent to a store in the interior, and to his great delight found himself close to "Bell's Creek Gold Diggings." Imagine a small Celestial of nine — active, smart, speaking a little pigeon English, just enough to make people understand he had come to look for gold, dressed in blue shirt and trousers, and a tiny cabbage-tree hat. No wonder the people of the store laughed at this minute gold-digger. Nothing daunted, however, little Quong persevered in his search for gold, and at the age of fourteen he had claims in which he was a sleeping partner, keeping one share and selling others. These claims multiplied, so that by the time he was twenty-eight he possessed the gold he coveted. So far all had gone well with him. Now his fortunes began to change. He lost some valuable horses, and his claims were worked at a loss to himself and the men employed.

It was noised abroad that luck had left Quong Tart, and, although things were not so bad with him as rumour had it, he no longer prospered. He had now to learn how ready people are to forsake the man who is not prosperous; so he watched this part of his career with interest, exaggerating his difficulties in order to see how his fellow men would behave to him. The men he employed called a meeting, and decided to leave him, after paying him a few empty compliments for his past generosity and kindness. He accepted their resignations, and went to his house and sat down to think. Presently three or four men came to the house, and said, "Look here, Quong Tart, your luck will turn again. We will stay with you another week." He thanked them, and after they had gone away, he took up a book sent to him by Mrs. Simpson, called "Line upon Line," and read in it the Story of Joseph, who had been sold into bondage, and passed through many hardships in a strange land amongst a strange people; but who had nevertheless risen to be a great man in Egypt.

He fell asleep, but woke up with a start, for he thought he heard someone speaking to him —

"Courage, Quong Tart; you shall yet be great," said the voice.

He jumped up feeling fresh and vigorous, and went to visit a claim. While examining a bit of ground already stripped he saw alluvial gold, and directed the men to dig further down. Presently a spade came up with gold sticking to it, and soon he was finding a half ounce of gold to the dish. His luck had come back again, and the men once more flocked to him.

But the crisis he had passed through had cured him of gold fever, and to the surprise of all at Bell's Creek he sold out.

Soon after this he went to China, and after a short visit returned to Sydney, where in 1881 he opened business as a silk and tea merchant.

Business was started on a very humble scale, a room in the Sydney Arcade being occupied for the purpose of selling dry tea. In order to advertise it, cups of it were supplied gratis at all hours of the day to all who cared to apply. So many availed themselves of the opportunity of tasting the delicious beverage that he decided to obtain larger premises where tea and scones could be served at a moderate cost. There are very few people, who, as they think of the vast number of tea and scone rooms in this great city of Sydney to-day, know that the one established by Quong Tart in the year 1881 was the first of its kind, no establishment of a similar character being existent there before that date.

The business increased by leaps and bounds and in the year 1885 he had opened no less than four places, and a number of large offices in the same Arcade.

The same year operations were extended to the Royal Arcade and the Pavilion at the Zoological Gardens, and, twelve months later refreshment rooms were started at 777 George Street.

At the close of the year 1889, after his second trip to China, it became necessary, in order to cope with the increasing trade, to open in King Street. The tea rooms were on a magnificent scale, the total cost of their establishment being six thousand pounds (£6,000). The patronage here, as at all his places, was splendid every day of the year. It was the management which won this patronage and nothing else. His employees were ordered to treat all alike, whether they wore silk dresses or cheap prints, for Quong Tart had long learned that the silk dress did not make the lady, nor the fine black coat the gentleman. Visitors got the best of everything served with conspicuous cleanliness and most courteous attention. Watchful management was present over every table and over every visitor.

On the first floor of the King Street premises a reading room was established, and tastefully supplied with journals and magazines of interest to ladies, also writing materials, so that if one desired to write a letter or address a parcel, the means were at hand, free of cost, and this great convenience was much appreciated by visitors.

But it was with the occupancy of the Queen Victoria Markets that his name as a city providore became famous. It was the biggest success in the line known in

Sydney. On the street floor he had a spacious and elegant well-served room, and upstairs was what was properly called the Elite Dining Hall and Tea Rooms. Taking the whole of these premises required a good deal of business courage, but the result as in the most of Quong Tart's undertakings showed the wisdom of the step.

The Elite Hall, from the very first day, was a decided success. A magnificent business was done and the "Elite" came to be recognised as the most elegant and best served dining hall in Sydney.

In addition to all this he still carried on an extensive trade in packet tea, which was imported direct, and sent unopened to the consumer. The trade mark in connection with the tea business was two hearts interwoven. When Quong Tart first started, it consisted of a single heart, but he soon found, per medium of a lawyer's letter, that in using this he was infringing the registered emblem of a "barbarian" tea merchant named "Love." The King Street Mandarin was by no means as "downy" then as he was in after years, and he was much put out at this misadventure. So he went off to consult his benefactor, Mr. J. H. Want, K.C., and that worthy, noticing his woebegone face, said, "Hullo, in trouble? Woman, eh?" "No," said Tart, "but I've lost my heart, and all through Love. But," said he, "when you lose one heart you should gain another, should you not?" "Logic," said Want. Then after Want had read the lawyer's note, Tart took a piece of paper from his pocket, on which was drawn a double heart, and said, "There, sir; in future my trade mark shall be two hearts instead of one, and closely interwoven."

Quong Tart was one of those who thought it far pleasanter to have a chop well cooked, daintily served by a well-apparelled waitress, with pretty surroundings, than to have it thrust upon one in a discourteous manner, and got up in any fashion. Accordingly his rooms were artistically arranged with marble reservoirs in which golden carp swam around, and ferneries designed in rock and virgin cork. Mirrors, hand-painted in Japanese art, were placed in every conceivable position, and these were relieved by massive Chinese wood-carvings in green and gold. Turn where one would there was a suggestion of coolness. Ferns, fountains, virgin cork, and water trickling could be seen, and hundreds of fans tempted the hot wayfarer to forget that the thermometer was among the nineties.

The rooms were replete with everything that the visitor could possibly wish for, in order to make himself comfortable, including a plentiful supply of lavatories, with hot and cold water laid on, writing rooms, luxuriantly furnished smoking rooms, and separate rooms for the accommodation of ladies.

No better proof of the excellence of the arrangements, the artistic manner in which the rooms were fitted up, and the perfection of the cuisine could be found, than the fact that the places were patronised by the best class of people in the city and from the country.

It was this genius for arrangement which contributed so largely toward the success of his business enterprise.

All things being equal, a genial personality counts for much in bringing to a prosperous issue any commercial undertaking, particularly of that character in which Quong Tart was engaged. His personal attractiveness disarmed criticism at all times, and won for him a large number of friends from among all classes. Those who patronised him were his friends first, and customers afterward.

This personal element entered largely into his dealings with his employees. There was none of that aloofness of spirit which so often keeps employer and employee apart. To get the best work out of his employees, he did not apply the pressure of the iron hand. Such a method fosters antagonism for each other, and produces class hatred and industrial revolt. Quong Tart saw that, "not through antagonism to each other, but through affection for each other," would the greatest material result be obtainable. Hence his employees were not looked upon as mere machines, to be driven at high pressure from one week's end to the other.

They were men and women with souls and were treated as such. Every opportunity was seized for developing a kindly feeling for one another, and cementing the ties which bound them together. The unanimity and good-fellowship that existed between him and those in his employ cannot be better described than by the old phrase of the happy family, of which Quong Tart was the father and adviser. They felt that he was one with them in their sympathies and desires, and they opened their hearts to him, and sought his counsel in all their difficulties. It is said by those who knew him best, "He never cursed employees when they made mistakes; he was too much of a gentleman for that, and he was lenient even to the point of overlooking a fault." So long as they conscientiously fulfilled their tasks, they had no fear of his disfavour. To keep in touch with them he adopted the method of holding social evenings and picnics for their entertainment. A pleasant harbour excursion or a musical evening arranged by him to which the employees and their friends were invited, served to promote good feeling and clear understanding between them.

Quong Tart recognised that in the business world it was not easy to be loyal to one's principles and preserve one's ideals unblemished. A temporary and seemingly unimportant tampering with principle may lead to considerable promotion of self-interests, whether it be in wealth, position or popularity, and the temptation to deflect from the right is great. But throughout his commercial career, morality and business were not divorced but united, and he never waved principle aside by saying "business is business." He combined the astuteness of the man of the world with the high principledness of the Christian, and so left behind an example that business men might profitably follow.

Speech Delivered by the late SIR JOHN ROBERTSON,
K.C.M.G., on the occasion of his presiding at
the opening of MR. QUONG TART'S new premises
in King Street, Saturday, December 21st 1889.

"Fill your teacups, gentlemen all. (Laughter.) I was under the impression that my days for presiding at any festive board were all over, and, in fact, I told my old friend Quong Tart three days ago that nothing would induce me to take the chair again. Now, however, I find myself in my old age committing a breach of promise (laughter), and I suppose I'll have to make the best of it, and that best will be but the best of a very bad bargain." ("No, no.")

Toasts of Queen and Governor honoured.

Sir John Robertson: Quong Tart, who is now a Mandarin of China, and consequently high in public life, like our worthy Governor, Lord Carrington, has been not only successful in doing good for himself, but to my knowledge during the whole of his career in Australia has done his very utmost for the Colony and its Colonials generally. (Cheers.)

Toast of the Evening.

Sir John Robertson: Again fill your teacups, or your glasses, friends and gentlemen. I rise to propose the toast of the evening, and that is "The Health of Quong Tart." (Loud cheers.) You all know him, and I'll pledge my word that not one of you know anything wrong of him. (Cheers.) Tart is no ordinary, jog-along-easy fossil of a slow-coach man. (Cheers.) He is a man who amongst the most abundant obstacles and against the worst and most trying difficulties has risen to a position of independence and high personal public esteem in this great city of Sydney, as well as throughout the length and breadth of Australia. (Loud cheers.)

I knew him when he was very, very young. He is young enough now for the matter of that (laughter); in fact, I knew him when he was a boy. Knew him when he was living in the home of that most estimable lady, Mrs. Simpson, sister of my learned friend, John Want, Q.C., M.P., and of Fred. Want. A more estimable man than he is not to be found. Of course he commenced life when young like all other men (laughter), but he commenced it with all the difficulties of being a foreigner (Hear, hear), and consequently with, to a certain extent, all sorts of popular prejudice against him; a prejudice which is very largely existent in these Colonies. Despite all that, he forced his way to the front, and has honestly earned the esteem of every man in the Colony whose esteem is worth having (Cheers.) There is no man more popular, or more singularly noted for his good citizenship, geniality and kindness than he. (Cheers.) He is known as well in the city as in the country, and I have known him to take a most active part in all charitable and public matters throughout the colony. He commenced his life, I believe, on the gold diggings at Braidwood at nine years of age. He was a smart young fellow with a head on him and a conscience in him, and, like most smart young fellows he got on.

I think I happened to be Colonial Treasurer when he landed as the bearer of a letter of introduction, the manuscript of which spoke of him in the very highest terms. He asked me to give him an introduction to the authorities in China and he took from me, and from the Governor of New South Wales, a letter bearing credentials to which I am proud to know and to say he was justly entitled, and to which he did every honour. (Cheers.) To no introduction did he do dishonour. He was received with every honour by the very highest in his own country — from the Emperor downwards, and as a result he was elevated to a Mandarinship. A few years ago he married in this country (Hear, hear.), and more than that, he married a most estimable young English lady. (Cheers.) And something more, he now has a beautiful and delightful little girl as a child (Cheers.), whose rearing in the family of a man like Quong Tart will be a guarantee of her becoming a lady estimable in the extreme. (Cheers.)

15

You all know of Mr. Tart's and Dr. Ong Lee's reception of and by the Chinese Commissioners during their late visit to Australia, and you know also of his many associations with public matters and private charities. (Cheers.) It is no use for me to try and enumerate them. I might go on for a long while, but it is enough to say that a man, and a stranger into the bargain, to have come amongst us and to have acquired the position and esteem which he holds must be a man with the ring of true steel about him, and an honest man into the bargain.

Now, gentlemen, charge your cups and your glasses, and drink heartily to the health and continued prosperity of our esteemed host and friend, Quong Tart. (Great cheering.)

Quong Tart's Visit to His Native Land.

It was a pretty, touching story Quong Tart used to tell of his visit to his native land; how the Queensland regulations were relaxed in his favour; with what distinction he was received by the Viceroy of Canton, and sent in the Viceroy's steam yacht, with a guard of honour to his native village; how, before the Imperial flag, all vessels gave place, all drawbridges opened, all custom house officers or squeeze station men held the hands and made obeisance; how the villagers were in fear and trembling at the unwonted sight of an approaching steamer bearing the emblems of the Viceroy; how their fears changed to rejoicing, when they found that the Mandarin she carried brought honour to his native village; how his old mother wept and laughed and wept again, when in the official who, in his robes of dignity, flung himself at her feet, she knew her absent boy; how he observed the rights for his father, who had not lived to see the happy day; how his relatives were made comfortable, and leading citizens received appropriate gifts, and how the feast was spread in honour of the ancestors, who, as in the good way of the Chinese, were through him ennobled.

Again, a few years later, he gratified the wish of his aged mother by taking home his wife and three children, that she might see them before she died.

"Gladly do we greet the return of our genial fellow-citizen, Quong Tart, to the land of his adoption, and earnestly do we hope ere long to see his name again among those charities to which he was so great a contributor. Among the pleasures, or rather should we say the greatest pleasure that attended his visit to his own land was the meeting with his aged mother, a circumstance from which a useful lesson may be learned by Australians. Quong Tart has brought back portraits of his father (we believe long since dead), and of his mother, both invested with marks of the dignity he now as a Mandarin bears. Honours gained in China do not, as with us, descend, but revert to parents, therefore are the parents of Quong Tart decorated. A lesson, we repeat, may be gained from this reverence for parents and respect to all." "Dawn," June 1st, 1889.

Quong Tart — Public Benefactor.

"Write me as one who loved his fellow men."

Quong Tart was essentially a man who loved his fellow men. This was his glory, that he loved them and was loved in return. Born with a great heart of love it was impossible that its lustre should be limited to the home, but that humanity outside should feel the warmth and cheer of its influence. His symapthy was as wide as human need and sorrow. All classes and conditions of men, all institutions worthy of help, came within the range of his benefactions, and there was scarcely a laudable object in the city or suburbs that he was not a prominent assister in. Indeed, his whole life was spent in doing little thoughtful acts which make life sweeter and men more united.

He was peculiarly gifted with that rare insight into human needs which enables one to offer succour before the piteous cry for help crosses the threshold of human lips. Just when failure stood facing many a man, the "genial Quong" came along, and without making the recipient feel he was in receipt of charity helped him out of his difficulty.

Compassion for men, especially for the sick and disabled in life's fierce battle, he certainly had, and that in an unbounded measure, but it was not of that kind which ends in the making of piteous appeals when occasion offers, but compassion which found its outlet in genuine and practical philanthropy. On one occasion, in the year 1885, he was asked, along with others, to speak at a treat given to the inmates of the Asylum for Women at the head of King Street. Speaking of that address a daily paper of that day said, "Mr. Tart's speech differed from that of others in that while they spoke high-sounding words, he determined to make the treat an annual affair," and this he afterwards attempted to do, not only for the unfortunates of that asylum alone, but for the indigent poor in the benevolent asylums of the State. How far he succeeded in this attempt may be seen by casually scanning the large list of institutions where every year such festivals were held.

Once convinced that he was doing the right thing, nothing could dissuade him from carrying it out. When reminded that many of the men in the asylums had no business there, that they had been fools and worse in their time, and did not deserve help, he would reply, "Yes, but the old boys have long ago done their evil, and suffered for it," and nothing gave him greater joy and satisfaction than the feeling that he had done all that now could be done for men who had suffered and sinned and been sinned against, and who had only to look forward to a court, which they might be allowed to hope would square the old boys' bills in the mercy that God knows which of us may yet need.

What welcomes he received on the occasions of those feasts! Who can describe them?

"When nearing the wharf on the day of the feast of the inmates of the Newington Destitute Asylum," says "The Echo" of 16th October, 1888, "Mr. Tart seemed suddenly seized with a fit; he waved his arms and rushed about the deck, shouting out to the old women how glad he was to see them. The moment they recognised who it was, the look of joyous gratitude that came over those wrinkled faces was worth going over from Sydney to see. The moment he reached the enclosure he was surrounded by the poor old creatures, who danced round and clapped their hands like children in a pantomime. 'Ah! God bless you for a good 'un. Mr. Tart!' 'The Lord preserve you and yours, dear Mr. Tart!' 'Have you brought Mrs. Tart?' and dozens of similar ejaculations, and when he told them Mrs. Tart would be there directly with the little 'Tart,' which they mustn't eat, their enthusiasm knew no bounds."

"Long time since I saw you!" "Now, you have a good bit of fun to-day, but don't flirt with the gentlemen from Sydney!" "How are you, Mary? I must have a dance with you when Mrs. Tart goes away," and similar expressions, with a kindly word for all, as he wended his way amongst them, raising his hat each time he shook hands with one of them, with as much grace as he would have done to his own wife.

It was no unusual sight on feast day at the asylums for his name to be blazoned forth with mottoes expressing welcome and thankfulness — "A Glorious Welcome to Quong Tart and His Friends!" "Vive Quong Tart le Grand!" "Will ye nae come back again?" were among the decorative mottoes at the Parramatta Asylum in 1886. Two years later, at the George Street Asylum, Parramatta, in honour of him, a Chinese flag which had evidently borne the battle and the breeze, waved all green and golden in the air, and the initials Q.T. were repeated at least a dozen times all over the place on shields. As he moved about among the inmates at the feasts, "God bless you," said out of hearts full of gratitude, was showered on him from every side. If blessings secure a happy hereafter for men, then surely in the world which lies beyond this, he has received a rich reward. How much his kindness and that of the noble committee he represented was appreciated, how much light it shed into the dark lives that already cast deep shadows into the misty recesses of eternity, none can foretell. The following is a portion of a poem of appreciation written by "An Old Inmate":–

"To the Ladies and Gentlemen and other Friends, who, through the advocacy of Mr. Quong Tart, have aided in their labour of love and liberality in giving the festival to the inmates of the Benevolent Asylums."

After expressing regret for the mis-used past, a past imperishable and never to be forgotten, he concludes:–

Hail! genial Quong Tart — foremost in the van
Of the earth's noble, who devised the plan
In thy philanthropy, thy love to man,
Full of compassion, with a heart aflame,
To feast the helpless poor, the blind, the lame;
Whose earnest zeal aroused each liberal heart
In this good cause to bear a willing part;
Who, blest with wealth, sought cheerfully to share
Of their abundance with the poor to spare;

Who through long years forgotten and unsought,
No friendly hand had e'er sweet comfort brought;
No friendly voice had cheered them on life's way,
Nor lit with sunny smiles their life's dark day.
In this new era of these brighter days,
Such kindly acts call forth our warmest praise.
Yet when the heart is full, words ill express
The depth intense of the heart's thankfulness.
Yet He Who spake as never man spake
Declared this truth for all mankind to take —
"That e'en a cup of water, freely given
For His sake, had its sure reward in Heaven."
So seeds of kindness sown, and each kind word,
Ne'er fell unfruitful nor escaped unheard;
And thus we pray that God may ever bless
Those true, kind friends who willed our happiness.
Again our thanks to all who've taken part;
Especially we thank Mr. Quong Tart.

Quong Tart was one of the members of the first Committee of the Hospital Saturday Fund, and when that day came round each year, he generously supplied the lady volunteer collectors with tickets, which enabled them to obtain refreshments, free of cost, at any one of his magnificent establishments.

Particular interest was manifested by him in the newsboys of this city (Sydney). He had always a kindly word for them, and as was his custom towards all, treated them in the most respectful and gentlemanly manner. Some of those boys, he thought, might possibly become the future leaders in our State, and he did honour to the capacity though not unborn, yet latent and unrevealed. In December of 1893 these boys to the number of two hundred and fifty were entertained by him at his Tea Rooms one Saturday afternoon. The youngsters first paraded the streets of the city, headed by the Croydon School Cadet Band, and displaying bannerettes indicating the names of the different newspapers of Sydney which they earn a livelihood by retailing. A little later found the boys seated at five long tables, on which were spread out a whole host of good things. As fast as the good things vanished, the waitresses appeared with fresh provisions, and in the end the boys had to confess that their efforts to clear the tables had altogether failed. After tea, a few able and instructive addresses were given by leading men, and the boys left the better for the tea and advice which had been tendered them.

Later on an entertainment of a similar character was given by him to the newsboys of Ashfield, Summer Hill, Croydon and Burwood.

In 1882 a terrible disaster occurred at the Bulli Colliery. A relief fund was opened, and Mr. Tart became a member of the committee. No service that he could render on behalf of those who had suffered in that disaster was withheld. As one of the promoters of the "Fancy Fair" in aid of the fund, he toiled assiduously to make it a great success. As a result of his energetic efforts, no less a sum than two hundred pounds was handed to the Mayor of Sydney as the first instalment of the proceeds.

The wreck of the E. and A. Company's S.S. Catherthun in August of 1895 furnished him with another opportunity of rendering assistance to those in need. The Catherthun struck on a reef, which is suposed to be a submerged patch, south of the Seal Rock Island. A south-westerly gale was blowing, heavy seas were running, and fifteen minutes after the first impact the ship settled down. The behaviour of the Chinese crew was simply admirable; they loyally stuck to their ship and obeyed orders, even though death might have been the result. It was suggested that something should be done to recognise their devotion to duty, and their efforts to save life after the foundering of the steamer.

Although a box of sovereigns, £1300 (uninsured) of Mr. Tart's was amongst the cargo, yet he at once forgot his own loss in the loss of others, and with the able assistance he rendered, the sum of one hundred and sixty-four pounds, five shillings was raised between Saturday morning and Monday night in aid of the crew, who suffered heavily by the wreck. On the evening prior to their departure for China, they were entertained by Mr. Tart at his refreshment rooms, Sydney.

But not only was he continually to the front in movements of a charitable character, but he also took an active part in work that made for the mental and moral development of the people.

In all ages we find many who have a deep interest in a few affairs; and many who have a superficial interest in many affairs, but few who have a deep interest in many affairs. Mr. Tart was certainly one of the few. Agencies to help the fallen he believed in, and assisted as far as he was able, but he never lost sight of the fact that prevention is better than cure, and any organisation that tended to uphold and strengthen character, and save manhood from disaster, could always count on his support.

A lover of children, he put forth every effort he could on their behalf. He pleaded their rights when they could not plead for themselves. Nothing aroused him to action more than the sight of children without a chance, born into conditions which militated seriously against their physical, mental, and moral progress. He claimed for them conditions where at least they should have the opportunity of commencing life with a character unsullied, and retaining, if not innocence, then that purity of heart upon which the security of individual and national life depends. As a member of the Child Study Association, his work on behalf of the children was referred to by the President, Dr. Carroll, as worthy of the highest praise and admiration. Expressive of their appreciation of his endeavours to make the lives of our girls and boys happier and sweeter, the Association requested him to accept, on behalf of his little daughter, Florence Gertrude, who was born almost simultaneously with its inauguration, a silver mug suitably inscribed, and at the same time conferring on her the honour of making her a life member of the Association.

During his presidency of the Waterloo Ragged School, he was also able to accomplish much good for the poor children of our city.

When resident on the Braidwood Goldfields, he erected at Bell's Creek a school and church at his own expense for the benefit of the European miners and their families.

While connected with the New South Wales Zoological Society, he erected and paid for its construction, a pavilion, where lovers of the cup that cheers might find their wants supplied. The "Han Pan," as it was called, was built of bamboo, prettily painted and dotted here and there with mystical symbols, which seemed to dodge one another in strangely grotesque fashion.

After having been in communication with the Chinese Imperial authorities for some time respecting matters affecting their native Empire and Australia, and in addition having received a semi-official request to visit China, he decided to accept the invitation, and at an early date took his departure. "During his visit there," says the "Sydney Morning Herald," "Mr. Tart made special inquiries relative to the prospects of opening up fresh markets there for Colonial produce. His first inquiry was directed to the trade in woollen goods, and in Hong Kong he found that fourteen large Chinese firms practically monopolised the soft goods import trade. He spoke to the leading men about introducing wool from Australia for purposes of manufacture, and found there was a consensus of opinion that the possibilities of the trade were great. Hitherto the trade had consisted principally of cotton goods, but woollen articles were greatly increasing in favour, and Mr. Tart was assured that if the industry were properly started there would be no question as to its ultimate success. It would have to be begun in a moderate way, as the trade needed to be worked up; but the manufacture would require British experts and machinery, while there would be an abundance of local cheap labour. If a factory were started on such lines as these, the Chinese merchants would readily become shareholders. Mr. Quong Tart was taken round by the Surveyor-General in a steam launch, and shown several suitable localities for a factory, and was assured that every facility would be afforded for the establishment of the industry. Tinned meat would not be acceptable as they would have to contend with the prejudice that exists against "dead" meat, but there is a splendid market for flour and preserved fruit, with a good market also for butter."

Thus, in securing such valuable information as this, he rendered a great service to the country as a whole.

As the years went by, the number of his benefactions increased. Time and money were spent in travelling about the city and country opening bazaars, flower shows, basket fetes, and village fairs. Missionaries for foreign fields, and Christian workers at home, representatives to Anglican Synods, Methodist Conferences, and Presbyterian Assemblies, influential visitors to Citizens' Congresses were generously entertained by him.

Never in his life was he slow to show his appreciation of any good work, and was always one of the first citizens to come forward on any occasion, irrespective of class or creed, to help in any movement which was for the general good. The greatness of his love, the breadth of his sympathy, the extent of his kindnesses cannot be fully ascertained. It is true that Mr. Tart's nationality was to some extent a barrier to a full appreciation of his life work, but, in the words of Henry George, I would say — Quong Tart or Joseph? What does it matter? The same deep and tender chords are stirred; and at the touch that makes the whole world kin, one cannot but feel ashamed of the bars, necessary though they may seem, that keep men apart. When the day of the truly "Superior Man" shall come, will they not cease to be?

Work on Behalf of the Chinese.

(General Outline).

What a wonderful personality Quong Tart possessed (although he belonged to that once despised Chinese Nation, which fact seemed to be an impossible barrier for even its most worthy sons to overcome amongst all the so-called Western civilised races); he was able, after a residence of nearly half a century to break down all the prejudices of all classes or creeds of the Anglo-Saxon race living in Australia, and also retaining the respectful and affectionate regard of his own countrymen. So popular did Quong Tart become in the community, that when a Levee was held at Government House he was sure to be there in his Mandarin costume to represent the land of his birth. If any striking event took place in China or with the Chinese in any part of the world, it was to Quong Tart the representatives of the press hastened for information, as he always kept in close touch with matters relating to his mother country. If a deputation of the Chinese was to be appointed to wait on the Government or Mayor, etc., or an address or petition presented, it was always Quong Tart who was entrusted with the management. When any distinguished men and women visited us from other countries (Missionaries in particular), Quong Tart entertained them well at his own cost, as well as the other guests whom he would invite to meet the visitors. To give an idea as to the popularity of Mr. Tart among the working classes alone — a well-known labour man was speaking in public and was pouring out his vials of wrath on "the wretched Chinese," "everyone of whom," he said, "he would, if he had his way, drive out of the State." "Would you do that to Quong Tart," cried out one from the crowd. "No, certainly not," replied the Labour orator. "If they were all as good as Tart, I would let them stay here and come here, as they would be sure to be good citizens." Notwithstanding the fact that the hero of this book was born in China and spent the tender years of his life in that country before residing in New South Wales, he was a British subject and a very loyal one, too, but it must also be added that he was always very strongly opposed to the imposition of the Poll Tax — believing, as he did, that as the Britishers were allowed all possible freedom in China so ought its people to be allowed the same freedom in Great Britain and her Dominions abroad, including "Sunny Australia." Many of our foremost public men have dared to say the same. The Rev. W. J. Williams, preaching at Auckland, championed the cause of the Chinese and with much eloquence pointed to Quong Tart of Sydney as a bright and shining example of all the virtues, and indignantly demanded, "How many Quong Tarts may we not be excluding from our shores by our hostile enactments?" As Quong Tart very frequently said, "It is not the vice of the poor Chinaman the public dislikes, but his virtues."

In 1887, the Anti-Chinese League stirred up the public feeling in this State. Quong Tart then pointed out how that the Chinese miners created wealth for the State as well as themselves, because they were content to search for gold in claims that had been abandoned by Europeans who had gone to try their luck on other fields. So, too, in regard to the competition of the Chinese in the furniture trade he very truly showed that in addition to providing the public, especially the poorer classes of our colonists, with attractive looking and well made furniture, and at a price much below what they had previously been asked to pay, they purchased the timber and all other materials needed in its manufacture from the Colonial Britishers. No one, he contended, would deny the statement that but for the Chinese our supply of vegetables would be very limited in the city and suburbs, or still more so in the country towns of this and the adjoining States of Australia.

Extract from the "Sydney Morning Herald," Friday, December 9th, 1887:–

On the Chinese Question.

By Quong Tart.

A few weeks ago I received a circular from the Secretary of the Anti-Chinese League of New South Wales, and feel I must write a few of my views on the subject, having lived in the Colony nearly all my lifetime, and been a British subject for nearly twenty years. I certainly would not have taken the slightest trouble to express any of my views whatsoever on the matter were it not for the absurd and extreme proposals made by this League, a few of the principal of which I will remark upon. £100 poll-tax. — Well, the treaty made between her Majesty and his Imperial Majesty in 1858 will decide that. The annual tax and license-fee of Chinese hawkers does not need commenting upon by me, for there are wise members in Parliament, who can deal correctly with that. Some of the Chinese say that "such a proposal looks like the league trying to be kind to the Government by making us pay, and so increasing the revenue; and they pick upon us because we are the weakest, having no one to defend us."

To a certain extent, I agree with the stoppage of naturalisation papers, but think they ought to be granted to any Chinese who is fairly known and well recommended by European and Chinese, and not to anyone who applies. The prohibition of Chinese from taking up any mine till it had been abandoned for three years reminds one of that little anecdote, "The dog in the manger." There are many instances of Europeans who have claims nearly worked out — in some cases completely worked out as far as the wages of Europeans is concerned — who, when they hear of a new rush, are off and sell their old claim or leavings to the Chinese for a certain sum, and in very few cases the Chinaman profits by the transaction. And were it to be left for a short time, for less than three years, it would be good for neither European nor Chinese, for it would be filled up or caved in, and would take quite £1 to make 19s. Then again, the Chinese often (because they have no chance only rarely to go into new rushes) work up the old tailings and drips of some old claim, making in many cases only from 15s. to 25s. a week; so did not they work up these leavings this wealth, as little as it is, would remain unfound, so that they ought not to be envied for their work, for no European would ever think of taking it up again. The prevention of Chinese from voting for Parliament or municipal is ignorant and prejudiced in the extreme. For what reason should not they be allowed to vote? Do not think that when they hear a man speak with good, sound, true principles they do not know it, for they do, and that well, too; and, although perhaps they cannot in English express their opinions, still they know (to put the matter short) a thorough gentleman when they meet him, and that is the man they vote for, whether he be in favour of Chinese here or not.

Upon certain firm and positive facts I declare that their Excellencies General Wong Yung Ho and Consul-General U Tsing did not, as this league supposes, visit these shores to spy out the land, and encourage immigration, for it is quite against the high authorities' rules to look after a mere sprinkling of their flock like there is in Australia. They were sent, through so many complaints about the poll-tax and other things reaching the ears of his Imperial Majesty, to inquire into and learn for themselves the true state of affairs concerning the treatment in general of all Chinese here before communicating with Her Majesty. I hold that the Chinese are as free to these shores as any other nation in the world, according to the treaty made.

This Anti-Chinese League, as a body, is very wise indeed to try and adopt plans to protect the labour of the Colony (did it need protection), and bring it into a thorough state of prosperity, and look for the future, and not for the present. But they should do it in such a manner as to not excite the larrikin element, for some are like a fuse ready for a (light) word to begin to molest the poor Chinese and make plenty of work for the Police Courts. I am sure that is far from the expectations of the principal gentlemen of the League, but such a thing will be, and is, and will cause the greatest of disturbance if not seen to in time.

In what labour do Chinese compete with Europeans? Not with coalminers, brickmakers, stonemasons, builders, wheelwrights, blacksmiths, shoemakers, tailors, roadmakers, Government contractors, &c., &c. — sailors, of course, already settled — but only in cabinet-making, the cultivation of the ground, gold-mining, hawking, general dealing, and fill up a few vacancies here and there, despised by Europeans. True, the cabinet-makers do, to a certain degree, compete with Europeans in this trade, but what harm could the present small number do among so many people? The timber and other necessary materials they require is bought from Europeans here, and they pay the same as any other person, so if they manage to sell cheap through their own economy people profit by it. Since this great agitation commenced, I have visited some of these cabinet warehouses and find the owners not rich, and in very many cases dispensing with their hands. The agricultural Chinese are a great saving of expense to the poorer class of Europeans, for they could not possibly get vegetables at all if Europeans alone had to cultivate them; they would have to pay, say, instead of 5s. for their greengrocery bill, 10s. Europeans would not so constantly work it, or even take such an interest in the work; therefore, could not make it pay like them, and would not think of having a garden at all unless water and every other convenience was close at hand; and there would not be nearly a sufficient number of Europeans to follow that pursuit to supply the population. Then, again, Europeans would not take the trouble to try and cultivate some of the sandy wastes, or even rocky ground, like the Chinese do; but would look for good soil, which they cannot always get. I think a wise plan for restriction would be, first to ascertain the number of Europeans and the number of Chinese in the Colony, then allow a certain number of Europeans to each Chinaman. By such means the land would not be over-run, for numbers leave yearly for China, so it would be more likely to decrease, and would save all this hum-bug of poll-tax outcries, &c., &c.

Some little time back a deputation waited upon the Minister for Works suggesting a special car to be put on the Botany tram line for the "dirty, nasty Chinese." Now, I think that were such a thing done for a time it would do good, that is, if all the dirty drunken Europeans (for they are a nuisance) were put into the same car as the Chinese, it would encourage cleanliness in both cases and be a comfort for other travellers, and would be the Englishman's motto, "Fair play," and would not make fish of one and flesh of another. For the keeping of sanitary and other laws among the Chinese, I humbly suggest for the Government to appoint about twelve capable Chinese men, each two to represent a province, as I think all Chinese here hail from about six provinces; also two religious men, to work in conjunction with a European inspector, to inquire into the condition, occupation, and general pursuits of every Chinaman in New South Wales, and for the Government to pay these men so much per annum and have elections each year; then enforce a law to make each Chinaman contribute 10s. yearly towards paying the expenses and making the commissioners' salaries a little higher, and any money over and above the expenses to go towards the building of a home for the old and sick Chinese, and be conducted and properly attended to by these same men, so that the old and sick would not be dependent upon the New South Wales Government. In reference to the common outcry against the Chinese decoying young girls away to their dens, I don't say that that race is an exception, but certainly the thing is much exaggerated. The whole firm foundation of this outcry originates from opium, and lies in the gambling and opium dens, and until these places are completely rooted out there will be a continuous outcry. The Anti-Chinese question is not so simple as some imagine, for unless it is amicably settled it might involve volumes of trouble.

In the same year, 1887, two Chinese Commissioners, General Wong Yung Ho and Consul-General U Tsing, visited Sydney, and Quong Tart introduced a deputation of the Anti-Chinese League, and the reply of the Commissioners interpreted by Quong Tart, was that "Neither the League nor the Colonists need fear any very great influx of Chinese to the Colony, as the Chinese did not do very well here, and many of them were worse off than they were in China, and stated that the competition was looked upon in China very much in the same light as the Chinese competition here, but they would give every consideration to the representation of the deputation." Many years have passed since this reply was given, and I think that even the members of the Anti-Chinese League, who are still living, will agree that the Commissioners were most truthful in their reply to that deputation.

During the stay of the Commissioners they showed keen interest in Quong Tart's efforts to put down and extinguish the opium traffic. They also stood as Godfathers to Quong Tart's eldest daughter, who was born at the time of their visit. The Commissioners took a large interest in a report furnished to the Government in 1884 by Mr. Tart and Mr. Sub-Inspector Brennan, who were appointed in the year 1883 by the Inspector-General of Police, with the approval of the Honourable the Colonial Secretary, to visit the various large Chinese camps in the Colony to make inquiry and report under the following headings, viz.:–

1. The population of each camp, conditions of occupancy, distinguishing Chinese, Europeans, and sexes.
2. Whether the children received any education and by what means.
3. The sanitary conditions of the camp and if sleeping accommodation were decent and sufficient.
4. How the Chinese obtain a livelihood.
5. What number of European women were married to Chinese.
6. How many were living in a state of common prostitution.
7. How many indulge in opium smoking.
8. To what extent gambling is carried on, and if European men and boys frequent the camp for that purpose.

It was after making that important inspection, Quong Tart found there was wide scope for good work from him to be done on behalf of his countrymen and those who associated with them; as the conditions disclosed then, all round were very bad. He directed his attention more particularly to the suppression of gambling and the use of opium — as once those two great vices were put down the smaller ones would lessen. His work on the opium curse will be found in another chapter.

In 1888 a burning Chinese question arose — the Anti-Chinese League had roused a few thousand people in Sydney against an imaginary influx of Chinese. Several ships had left Hong Kong with a few hundred Chinese on board for the Colonies, under the then Poll Tax, agreement. The League imagined "the stream had commenced to flow" and as the League "was pledged to check any further immigration of Chinese by all legitimate means" there the trouble came in. A big question arose — these Chinamen were on their way — so meetings were held at the Town Hall, "scenes of excitement took place at the Parliament buildings, and it was feared at one time the Legislative Chamber would be invaded by the irate mob:" the outcome of it all being — the passing of a Drastic Chinese Restriction Bill, in all its stages, in one night, by the Government, headed by the Premier, Sir Henry Parkes, its effect being to prevent any of these Chinamen from landing. When the steamers arrived in the Harbour the men on board were informed 'A new Law' had been passed since they had left their homes and they would have to return without even the slightest redress. Imagine how they felt against such an injustice!

Quong Tart set to work — he was determined to see what he considered a big wrong righted, as some of the men on board were British subjects. He with several leading Chinese merchants and others toiled night and day, and eventually succeeded after much trouble and with the aid of the Judges of the Supreme Court in getting the law modified, and forty per cent of the men landed who had come under the existing law at the time of their leaving China. Some of the Chinamen sent back were not legally entitled to land as their papers were incorrect and in some cases forged — so, of course, they were forced to return sadder but wiser. Quong Tart was justly proud of his mediation at that time and hundreds of his countrymen thanked him for his wise intervention. The following is an extract from the "Sydney Daily Telegraph" of September 5th, 1888:–

The Chinese Question.
Views of the Chinese Ambassador.
The Agitation a Political Trick.
(Our Special Messages.)

London, Monday Night. — Mr. Randolph Want, who is now in England, is forwarding to Mr. Quong Tart, of Sydney, certain proposals of the Chinese Ambassador with respect to Chinese emigration to the Australian colonies.

London, Tuesday. — The "Times" of this morning devotes an article to the Chinese restrictive legislation which is being passed by the Australian colonies and declares that the anti-Chinese agitation in Australia is the outcome of a political trick.

The following is an extract from the "Sydney Daily Telegraph" of May 6th, 1889.

"Mr. Tart is the first prominent Chinese merchant who has visited the Celestial Empire since our international troubles of 12 months ago. It was therefore interesting to hear his opinion of the temper in which he found the people of that country concerning our decision, in putting a stop to their Australian pilgrimages. He says that we can form little idea of the anger that was manifested by the masses in Hong Kong and Canton upon the return of the ships with the rejected immigrants on board. Many of the unfortunate people were landed in their native country in a state of utter destitution. What little they had possessed before embarking on the eventful voyage had been sold to supply the needs of ready cash, and in most cases they had had recourse to the tender mercies of moneylenders, whose rates in China are as high as they are anywhere else in the world. Thus, when they landed after their enforced trip back they formed a rather striking illustration of the manner in which Australia had come to regard the question of Chinese immigration. Their want and destitution appealed to the sympathies of their countrymen and their stories of imprisonment on board the ships in Sydney Harbour inflamed the popular anger."

In 1897 the Alien Bill was again before the House. One clause was highly objectionable to the Chinese merchants, so Quong Tart was empowered by the

Chinese residents of the city to endeavour to get the clause struck out. With that object in view he was allowed to address the Upper House — the clause being afterwards amended. Petitions to Parliament he was not infrequently called upon to prepare and have presented. The following is a copy of one in the year 1897:–

New South Wales.
Legislative Council.
Coloured Races Restriction and Regulation Bill.

(Petition from Quong Tart, praying the House to so amend the Bill as to grant leave to Chinese Merchants to make business visits to the Colony.)
(Presented by Sir A. Renwick, 30th November, 1897.)
Printed Under No. 6 Report from Printing Committee.

The Honourable the President and Members of the Legislative Council of New South Wales, in Parliament assembled.
The petition of Quong Tart, Chinese Merchant, resident in New South Wales:–

Humbly Showeth —
1. That your Petitioner is informed and believes that a Bill "To apply and extend certain provisions of the Chinese Restriction and Regulation Act of 1888 to other coloured races, to amend the said Act, and for other purposes incidental to, or consequent upon, the before-mentioned objects," is now under the consideration of your Honourable House.
2. That a deputation of the Chinese resident in New South Wales waited upon your Petitioner this day, and requested your Petitioner to make the representations contained in this Petition, on behalf of the Chinese so resident as aforesaid, to your Honourable House, and to pray for the relief hereinafter specified.
3. That the Chinese residents in New South Wales are a peaceable, law-abiding, and industrious class of residents, whose residence in the colony is conducive to the production and expenditure of wealth within the said colony, as appears from the following facts, which may be verified from official statistics:–

(a) That the number of Chinese in gaol in the said Colony bears a much lower percentage to the whole number of Chinese resident in the said Colony than is the case in respect of any other nationality.
(b) That of the Chinese male population resident in the said Colony nearly sixty-two in every hundred are primary producers of wealth, whilst of the whole male population of the said Colony, only twenty in every hundred are primary producers of wealth.
(c) That the Chinese resident in the said Colony expend annually not less than £250,000 or about £18 per head in food and clothing of European or Australian production, in addition to about £8 per head of goods produced in and imported from China.

4. That the Chinese merchants, who have businesses established in the said Colony are under great disadvantage and hindrance in carrying on their business by reason of the fact that the Chinese Restriction and Regulation Act of 1888 makes no provision for the exemption from the provisions of that Act of merchants who may require to go from New South Wales to China on business with the purpose of returning to New South Wales again, or who may require to come to New South Wales from China on business with the purpose of returning to China again.

5. That the Chinese merchants who desire to make such visits as aforesaid would, as a general rule, only need to visit New South Wales or China respectively for a very short period, and that, as a general rule, the exigencies of their business would prevent them from making prolonged visits; but that in certain cases it is necessary for some Chinese merchants to make a prolonged visit for the purpose of winding up their said business, or for examining into and re-organising the affairs thereof.

6. That not only in the interests of the Chinese merchants, but also in the interests of the business of the said Colony with China, some amendment of the Act above-mentioned should be made to enable Chinese merchants to make such visits as aforesaid without being subject to the provisions of the said Act

Your Petitioner, therefore, humbly prays as follows:–

1. That your Honourable House will be pleased to insert in the Bill mentioned in paragraph one of this Petition, some provision for enabling Chinese merchants to make such visits as are specified herein without being subject to the provisions of the Chinese Restriction and Regulation Act of 1888.

2. That your Honourable House will be pleased to extend such provisions to such other class or classes of Chinese residents as to your Honourable House may seem just and expedient.

And your Petitioner, as in duty bound, will ever pray, &c., &c.

QUONG TART.

Dated at Sydney this 30th day of November, 1897.

The Chinese Problem or Question, during Quong Tart's life, to be fully explained and showing the part he always played in it, would form a very lengthy and interesting volume in itself.

One of the high marks of distinction bestowed upon him during his long residence in New South Wales was when, in the year 1890, the late Sir Henry Parkes, as Premier of this Colony, appointed him (Quong Tart) to act as a member of a Royal Commission, "to make a diligent and full inquiry with a view of ascertaining the undoubted facts in the matter of alleged illicit gambling and immoralities among the Chinese residents in George Street North, in the said City of Sydney and neighbourhood, and the alleged bribery or misconduct of any members of the Police Force in relation thereto; also to make visits of inspection to localities in the said City and Suburbs occupied by Chinese, and investigate and report upon social conditions, means of sanitary provisions in the dwellings and workshops, the callings or occupations and other circumstances affecting the well-being of such persons."

With Quong Tart on this Royal Commission were Sir W. P. Manning, the then Mayor of Sydney, Mr. J. S. Hawthorne, and Mr. Francis Abigail, for some years members of the New South Wales Parliament, and Mr. Ramsay McKillop, a well-known Labour leader.

In the early part of the year 1892 the Royal Commission sent in its report to the Government of New South Wales. A perusal of the questions and replies in this very bulky but interesting report would show what a useful part Quong Tart played in this very important Royal Commission.

A very amusing incident occurred at one of the sittings of the Commission when a Chinese witness, of that country's larrikin type, was being examined as to his well-known connection with some of the gambling dens, stating "that several of the leading Chinese merchants were interested in the gambling shops, and that a cousin of Quong Tart also had several shops, and that it was believed that this latter gentleman had an interest in them also." When Quong Tart heard this he became indignant and gave the statement a flat denial. One of the other members of the Commission questioned the witness on this vile accusation, and obtained from him replies that the ground for his statement was that he and others had seen Quong Tart go into this so-called cousin's business premises on several occasions, and when asked how Quong Tart was related to the man so as to be called a cousin, replied, "He comes from the same part of China as Quong Tart, and we call him a cousin." Then the question was put, "If Quong Tart, say, came from Pekin, every Chinaman living in Sydney who came from the same part would 'all be cousins.'" His reply was "Yes," and to a further question he stated that he believed Quong Tart to be an honourable man, and that he was held in great favour by all respectable Chinese, and that personally he did not believe that Quong Tart had any interests or sympathy in Chinese gambling.

In 1896 he was the leader in the movement to return about twenty-one Chinese lepers from the Little Bay Lazarette to their homes in China (for inherent in all Chinese is that extreme desire to spend the last days of their lives among their own kith and kin), so he collected money from his compatriots to defray their expenses, and gave much time and labour to the completion of all necessary arrangements to get them safely away, with the assistance of the Government and small publicity to the public.

It is nearly twenty years since the Chinese faction fights took place in Sydney, and as a result many of the startling incidents that happened then have been forgotten, but a look through the Sydney daily papers in the early part of the year 1892 will show what a leading power the late Quong Tart (as mediator) was among the Chinese of all classes in this State, as also those of the adjoining States, and this position he maintained up to the day of his death. Those who knew him intimately whether they were Chinese or British would testify how anxious he was at all times to improve the conditions of the everyday life of his countrymen, and how ready he was to defend them when they were subjected to any unfair criticism or unjust or ungenerous treatment. This striking trait in Quong Tart's character was recognised by the wealthy, as well as the labouring class of Chinese in New South Wales. They knew that if they were acting unwisely or in any way affecting their good position as citizens he would reprove them to their face, but he was always prepared to stand forth in their defence when detraction was aiming its deadly weapon at their reputation. It was their wish, as also that of many others, that he should be appointed the first Chinese Consul for Australia as a slight recognition of his devotion to and work for China and its sons in this part of the world. The following are the signatures of the Consuls resident in Sydney, New South Wales, asking the Chinese Government to appoint Quong Tart as first Chinese Consul-General for Australia.

Added to this is a request to the same authority from some of the leading men of the Commonwealth, headed by the then Prime Minister, also suggesting that Quong Tart should be appointed Consul-General for China in Australia.

Sydney, New South Wales, Australia, February 3rd, 1903.

We, the undersigned Consular representatives of Foreign Powers stationed in Sydney, can certify to the position held by Mr. Quong Tart among the Chinese and Europeans here during our terms of office.

China has no Consul in this State, and the Chinese community being fairly large, there are necessarily frequent calls upon Mr. Tart to perform the duties that would otherwise fall to their official representative had they one here. He is their recognised spokesman in all matters, and is esteemed and respected by all classes and nationalities resident in the State, and should be able to represent his country as Consul.

GUS. BIARD D'AUNET (Consul-General of France to the Commonwealth of Australia).

PAUL VON BURI (German Consul-General).

H. EITAKI (Acting Consul-General for for Japan).

ERNEST W. T. DUNN (Vice-Consul for Brazil).

TH. AUG. BOESEN (Consul-General, Denmark).

ORLANDO H. BAKER (Consul of United States of America).

A. SCHEIDEL (Consul of Austria-Hungary).

CHEVALIER DR. V. MARANO (Vice-Consul for Italy).

GEORGE F. WILLIAMSON (Consul for Ecuador).

FRANK R. FREEHILL (Consul for Spain).

EDMUND RESCH (Consul Netherlands).

W. H. PALING (Vice-Consul Netherlands).

JAS. T. TILLOCK (Consul-General for the Argentine Republic).

WILLIAM BROWN (Consul for Chile).

J. S. LARKE (Agt., Govt. Canada).

THOMAS HUGHES BARLOW (Acting Consul for Greece).

OLAV E. PAUSS (Swedish and Norwegian Consul for New South Wales and Queensland).

E. M. PAUL (Consul for Russia).

MARC RUTTY (Consul for Switzerland).

J. CURRIE ELLES (Vice-Consul for Belgium).

Sydney, N.S.W., Australia,
February 2nd, 1903.

We, the undersigned, can testify that Mr. Quong Tart has resided in our midst for upwards of 20 years, and has, during that period, possessed the confidence and esteem of the entire community.

His aim has ever been for peace, and he is always ready and willing to act as mediator when disputes or misunderstandings arise between the Chinese and Europeans — these occasions being of no infrequent occurrence in the earlier days on the goldfields — and his intervention has invariably been the means of effecting a satisfactory settlement. In many important cases he has been requisitioned by the Government to act as interpreter, and was appointed to a seat on a Royal Commission by the Government, of which the late Sir Henry Parkes was head.

Mr. Tart's services to the Chinese poulation here are widely known, for having no Consul to whom they can look for information, or redress for their grievances, they invariably appeal to him as their recognised spokesman and representative in this State.

On all sides and by all classes and nationalities, Mr. Quong Tart is highly respected, and his popularity was strikingly manifested by the unprecedented and spontaneous outburst of sympathy with him from every quarter of the Commonwealth on the occasion of the murderous attack to which he was recently subjected.

His best endeavours are, and always have been, devoted towards securing better conditions, politically and socially, for his countrymen, and his efforts have been unceasingly directed towards their advancement and general welfare.

EDMUND BARTON (Prime Minister).
ARCHD. H. SIMPSON (Judge of Supreme Court).
WILLIAM JOHN LYNE (Federal Home Secretary).
EDMUND FOSBERY (Inspt.-Genl. of Police).
RT. HON. G. H. REID, Q.C. (Leader of Opposition, Federal Parliament).
WILLIAM McCOURT Speaker, Legislative Assembly, N.S.W.).
THOMAS HUGHES (Lord Mayor of Sydney).
DAVID KIRKCALDIE (Railway Commissioner of New South Wales).
G. B. SIMPSON (Justice of the Supreme Court of New South Wales).
R. E. O'CONNOR (Vice-President of the Federal Executive Council).
JOHN SEE (Premier, State New South Wales).
F. LOCKYER (State Collector of Customs, N.S.W.).
CRITCHETT WALKER (Principal Under Secretary).
SYDNEY SMITH (M.H.R.).
M. H. STEPHEN (Acting Chief Justice).
HORACE JOHNSTON (Merchant, President Chamber of Commerce).
WM. OWEN (Judge of Supreme Court).

BRUCE SMITH (M.H.R., Barrister-at-law).
H. E. COHEN (Judge of the Supreme Court of New South Wales).
SIR JULIAN SOLOMONS, K.C.
W. M. FEHON (Railway Commissioner).
ROBERT D. PRING (Judge of Supreme Court).
JOS. CARRUTHERS (M.L.A., Leader of Opposition, New South Wales).
GEORGE R. DIBBS (Ex-Premier New South Wales).

Clipping from Sunday "Truth":–

"'Truth' understands that the Government at Pekin has had the question of appointing a Consul-General for Australasia brought under its notice more than once, and we are decidedly of opinion that if the Ministry of the day were to let it be known, of course through the proper official channels (Chinese officials being great sticklers for etiquette), that New South Wales (and, indeed, Australia generally) would be glad if such an appointment were made, and would willingly accord official recognition to the gentleman chosen, an arrangement would speedily be arrived at. The present war affords a splendid opportunity for pushing Australian business in the East. New South Wales produces some of the best coal in the world for steaming purposes, and for the purposes of war the very best coal is of supreme, vital importance. Directly its enormous army is placed on a war footing, China must import large quantities of silver in order to pay her soldiers, and here again New South Wales steps to the front. In like manner, our copper and tin would be readily absorbed by the powerful Celestial Empire, while, so long as the war lasts, there will be an increased and ever-increasing demand for Australian tinned and preserved meats. A Consular representative of China, living in Sydney, would be able to see that none but the very best articles of their kind were purchased for the purpose required, for, if inferior coals or bad provisions were once supplied, the trade would vanish, probably never to return. In this connection it is worthy of note that in Mr. Quong Tart we have a resident in our midst able to fill this responsible position alike with credit to himself, to the satisfaction of Australians generally, and to the equal satisfaction of the great Empire which he would, we feel sure, so worthily represent. We happen to know that Mr. Tart (whose business qualifications and whose character for commercial probity and rectitude so completely fit him for the post) would be 'persona grata' at the Court in Pekin. He has visited the Chinese Empire thrice since he founded his present business; he bears an honourable reputation, both in Australia and China; and his appointment would be acceptable to the political and commercial magnates of this country, as well as to the Court officials of the Empress Dowager at Pekin. Under these circumstances, therefore, we urge upon the Ministry the advisability of the Colonial Secretary taking immediate steps to get China properly represented here, and at the same time bring the claims of Mr. Quong Tart under the notice of the Imperial authorities. This could probably be done by cable, and the appointment fixed up as soon as possible."

It may be asked by someone who was not acquainted with the useful noble life of Quong Tart, why so much enthusiasm was displayed by so many of our leading public men in having him so honoured by the rulers of that mighty nation from which he sprang — the answer is simply this, that for many years he did so much work for his country and countrymen as to win for himself the title "The unpaid Consul-General for China," and I have the assurance of an Australian friend, who visited London some time after Quong Tart's death, that she met in one of the leading Tourist Hotels of that great city, a worldwide known literary man who had been the representative in Pekin, China, of one of the leading daily papers of London, who, in the course of conversation, when Quong Tart's name was mentioned, stated that he knew as a fact that just at the time the cable messages to Pekin arrived announcing his (Quong Tart's) unexpected death, the official papers were going through the Government Departments of the Chinese Capital appointing him to the important position of "Consul-General for the Chinese Empire in Australia." How sad to think that just as he had almost clasped the reward of his lifelong labours in his hand —

"All was ended now, the hope, and the fear and the sorrow;
All the aching of hearts, the restless unsatisfied longing;
All the dull, deep pain and constant anguish of patience."
— Longfellow.

Views and Work on the Suppression of Opium.

When Quong Tart was leaving home in the year 1859 he promised his father that, come what would, he would never indulge his taste in opium. Returning after a residence of twenty-five years in Australia, he was able to say to his aged sire, "Father, I have kept the promise I made to you. Since I left your care I have not tasted opium." The old man's heart bounded with joy, for he was one who had ever been zealous in endeavouring to shake from his countrymen that hideous curse, opium smoking, and his hope had ever been that the force of his example might save his children. Truly a great hope and treasured throughout the many years, and which as the foregoing lines reveal found its full fruition in his son's zealous devotion to a vow made when, as far as years count, he was but a lad. Not only did he refrain from using opium himself, but a very considerable portion of his time was devoted to an heroic attempt at its entire suppression.

In order that the reader may understand fully the reasons of the attitude taken by Mr. Tart in connection with this evil, it will be necessary to give just here a brief outline of what opium is and some of its results.

Definition: "Opium is a stimulant narcotic poison which may produce hallucinations, profound sleep, or death." The successive use of it tends to impair the mental, moral and physical systems, and the greatest of vices — indolence, indency and immorality follow closely in its train. It has the effect of casting a wondrous spell over its victims, and is a habit from which it is almost impossible to be freed.

"Opium is one of the most powerful and useful drugs known to science, and is in that sense a great blessing to mankind. Regarded in another light, it is a curse. It is a means of dissipation more seductive, more insidious in its growth, and more terrible and degrading in its effects than anything else that can be named. The apparently hopeless drunkard may be reclaimed. In fact, it is hard to say when a case of drunkenness is altogether hopeless. But there is a stage too well known to thousands of victims, when the opium smoker is beyond human aid, and may well be allowed to have nothing good or useful left to him to do on earth. The only hope in connection with his miserable life is that he may not leave behind him, in perpetuation of his being, some ghastly caricatures of the Divine Law. If alcoholic indulgence insensibly grows upon men until they become pronounced dipsomaniacs, it may be said that opium smoking is a thousand times more insidious in its influence. The miserable victim of it is no longer a responsible being. He is a wreck, a ruin, and has sunk lower than the meanest specimen of God's creation. Once the opium pipe is touched, and ever afterwards, to the victim's dying day, the drug is more a necessity of life than food itself. The soul is chained with the first taste of the tyrant drug, and though there are instances of the abandonment of opium using, these are but as one in ten thousand to the cases where the chain has ever strengthened its links right down to the grave. Once let a man touch the opium pipe, and he becomes by turns a thief and maniac. Let a woman taste opium, and she becomes — let it not be written, part of the degradation can be imagined, the other part cannot be realised, even when her fate is seen, her habits regarded."

Such are the opinions of eminent men on this evil.

It is curious that the first blow struck at the iniquitous traffic in New South Wales should have come from the Chinese themselves, who were the chief consumers of this dreadful drug.

Quong Tart, with the sound of his father's voice still ringing in his ears, and the memory of a vow made in early days still distinct, and knowing the power of opium to blast the brains, ruin the body and destroy the soul, originated a crusade against it. It was no hearsay knowledge he had of the subject. He had seen for himself its dire effects, and his soul was stirred with pity and with anger. With pity for the victims whose intelligence and chastity fell down before its hideous power: with anger that a country calling itself Christian should allow a soul-destroying and character-beggaring drug to be imported into our midst. He had breathed the spirit of the great Chinese Emperor who, when asked by the British to legalise the trade, replied, "It is true I cannot prevent the introduction of the flowing poison. Gain-seeking and corrupt men will, for profit and sensuality, defeat my wishes, but nothing will induce me to derive a revenue from the vice and misery of my people."

And so while the instituted authorities were living in comfortable ignorance of a great danger at their very doors, there was kindling a spark in the heart of one noble man — and he a foreigner — which led ultimately to the evil being consumed, and thus the cause of much social degradation was removed.

Moral passion and purpose ran high within him, as he viewed his own countrymen, and the people of his adopted country, too, led by opium to indulge in vice clothed in its most hideous forms, shamelessness and immorality utterly beggaring description; men and women upon whose pure souls God had stamped the fair image of Himself, giving themselves over to the commission of the most beastly sins, in which the violent passions are lit and allowed to burn, gambling and other exciting pleasures pursued until the nerves began to wince, and the frame to totter from the excessive stimulation.

With such an agent for mischief in our midst, whose octopus-like influence was ever ready to entrap the unthinking and the young, no wonder that all that is best and truest and most sacred in humanity should rise up within him in moral protest against that spirit of lethargy which allowed it to exist.

With the same lofty motives which have actuated the devoted toilers in all ages, in the cause of justice and truth, as against injustice and oppression, he set out to arouse the moral consciousness of the people, and to create a public opinion which would demand in the interests of manhood and nationhood the abolition of the importation of opium.

The task he undertook was no easy one. The Chinese (mostly those of the gambling class) have a love for this insidious compound, and their dull phlegmatic temperaments do not offer a very promising field for the reformer to work upon. Besides the revenue derived by the State as duty was a large and ever increasing one, and to persuade the Government of the country to forego this was a difficult thing indeed.

But so well were his energies applied that before long the question was forced into a prominent position amongst the big social questions of the day.

In 1881 he took a trip to China, where he studied the question in its effect upon his countrymen there, as well as upon the Europeans. He found that though extensively used by the poorer classes, amongst the upper classes there was comparative freedom from the drug.

Two years later he was appointed to accompany Sub-Inspector Brennan on a visit to the various Chinese camps in New South Wales, the object of the visit being to ascertain the conditions prevailing in them.

The investigation revealed that the principal cause of their unsatisfactory state — moral and sanitary — was opium. In his report furnished to the Inspector-General of Police in November 1883, he says "That the fulcrum on which rests all vice, immorality and corruption with the Chinese, is opium. To it, the ills arising from the Chinese and their camps can be traced, and it is only by placing that detestable drug beyond the reach of my countrymen that the Government of the State can hope for reformation. In view of the importance attached to this particular part of the investigation I made it my business to make special inquiries at each camp to test the feelings and opinions of consumers on the matter, and I found that of the great number who indulged in opium smoking nine-tenths admitted the necessity of reform, and declared their willingness to sign a petition calling upon the Government to stop the importation of opium into the State, in quantities beyond that which may be required for medicinal purposes. Then, if the Chinese themselves are willing, and in fact anxious that the importation of opium be stopped, and if it can be shown that so much baseness arises from it, the Parliament of the country will not hesitate to pass a measure which will have that effect."

"I find from the Customs' Statistics that last year the quantity of opium imported into the State was 25,922 lbs. On this enormous quantity a duty of 10/- per lb. was levied, which adds the very considerable sum of £12,961 to the revenue of the state. We will not be far wrong in assuming that four-fifths of this was consumed by the Chinese, and if we take into consideration the number of Chinese in the State, the consumption per head is alarming, not only on account of the wretchedness and poverty brought upon the Chinese themselves, but because their example will be copied by Europeans, and must have a dire effect upon many who might otherwise become useful and worthy citizens. In this very city may be found many Europeans fast giving way to its infatuating influence, men unable to satisfy their cravings with intoxicating liquors, youths ignorant of its awful results, women who by its degrading influences descend to the lowest depths of depravity. If stronger evidence than this is required, we have the result of our late investigations. Out of seventy-three European women found in the camps visited, more than fifty were habitual smokers. Is this fact alone not sufficient grounds for prohibitive legislation?"

Immediately on the presentation of this report he took steps to lay the matter before the Government. A deputation was formed to wait upon its head, and they presented a petition in favour of the suppression of opium smoking, which was signed by seven hundred and sixty-eight municipal councillors, ministers of all denominations, two thousand five hundred European citizens, and five hundred Chinese.

On the 24th of April, 1884, the interview took place, the late Sir Alexander Stuart and Sir George Dibbs receiving the deputation. Sir Alexander Stuart told them that while he sympathised with their object, he could not help thinking that were the drug not imported it would be smuggled, and consequently the smoking would not cease, while the Government would lose the revenue.

But previous to this Mr. Tart had visited Victoria in furtherance of the movement, and found the large majority of the public there, especially in Ballarat, heart and soul with them.

Subsequently, Sir George Dibbs, who took great interest in the question accompanied him in a tour of inspection round some of the 'dens' where the smoking was indulged in, and he saw for himself how it was getting hold of the unfortunate people.

Unfortunately however, owing to some change of Government the matter dropped.

In 1887, he published a pamphlet entitled "A plea for the abolition of the importation of Opium." At the end of this chapter is the copy of the pamphlet in which he conclusively showed that the constant use of opium impaired the moral and physical systems, increased the gambling and criminal propensities of the Chinese and caused them to assemble in ill-ventilated and crowded apartments, and that girls and women after using the narcotic became habitues of evil resorts.

In November, 1890, he succeeded in bringing the subject under the notice of Sir Henry Parkes, but again with no definite result. Nothing daunted, he kept up the agitation, and at last a large and enthusiastic public meeting, convened by him, with the object of urging upon the Government the immediate necessity for restricting the sale of opium, was held on Thursday, April 5th, 1894, in the Congregational Church, Pitt Street, Sydney. The Church, which had been beautifully decorated, was crowded to excess in every part, and the proceedings throughout were strongly marked by earnest enthusiasm. Only those who were present at that meeting can adequately describe it. The appearance or Miss Ackerman (World's Missionary, W.C.T.U.), Dr. Storie Dixon, and Mr. Tart was greeted with loud applause, the audience rising in masses and waving their handkerchiefs.

Mr. Tart's speech on that occasion deserves to be placed on record as one of the greatest ever made on the subject in Australia. The deep feelings he had long cherished on the subject found adequate expression in an utterance which thrilled the audience to a man. Philanthropist, Reformer, and Humorist stood alternately revealed. Direct, personal, practical, liberally crammed with lofty sentiments from its beginning to its close it wrought a profound impression in the mind of every hearer.

On that occasion he said: "He could not help thinking that if ever the citizens of any country spoke out on any subject, that great meeting with its unanimous voice would say most unmistakably that the opium traffic must cease (cheers). There were, no doubt, people who thought the drug harmless, and the smoking of it fraught with little danger, but let them wait till the shoe pinched (cheers); let them wait till it touched their own daughters or their own sons. (Loud applause) That was the time they found the pinch, and that was the time when the evil came to close quarters — that it touched their hearts. He had no animosity against anyone on the subject. He was actuated purely by a desire to see the best done that could be devised to ameliorate the lot of the unfortunate victims, and prevent them falling under the fatal spell. Since he had taken the organisation of this meeting in hand, he had been almost besieged with letters of sympathy and encouragement from all parts of the State. Ministers of religion, leading politicians, municipal bodies, and prominent citizens in every walk of life had combined to wish the movement God-speed. He had received all these (holding up a huge bag packed with letters) within a fortnight. Where then could be the difficulty in stamping out this evil? There was no difficulty at all. (Cheers.) He would send out a full list of these communications all over the world to let people see what Australia thought of the traffic. Who could stand out of such a movement with clean hands? The deadliness of the drug would be realised when it touched their own kith and kin.

"Some forty or fifty years ago there was a Viceroy in China named Sum Tak Tooz, who took a great interest in this question. He went round the country and the cities and saw the degradation and misery which was settling down upon the people owing to this habit, and at once set himself to try and remedy the evil. He built large bamboo houses, or hospitals as they would be called here, for the treatment of smokers, he tried in every way to wean them from the habit. He also placed a law upon the Statute Book making it a capital offence for anyone to commence the indulgence. Not long after this his only son was decoyed away from him, and induced to smoke by some people who thought that the Viceroy would alter his decision when he found his own son's life involved. But it was ordered to stand, and the result was that the Viceroy signed the death warrant of his only son, as an example to the rest of the people. Surely here was a high and noble example to set to the world. Could mortal man show his fellows the imminence of their peril, and could one possibly find out a stronger argument in our favour than this? He thought not. But even the sacrifice of an only son had but a passing effect upon the opium scourge. The unfortunate Viceroy never lived to report the matter to the Emperor, and a further stimulus was given to the traffic from outside, and from no other source than "Christian England." (Cries of shame) Their dear old mother country poured shipload after shipload of the drug into China, and the Chinese were powerless to stop it. They were not strong enough to risk the chances of another war, should they repudiate the commercial treaty with England; and although a noble effort was made to prevent the iniquitous importation, it ended unfortunately, and China sat down meekly under the defeat. I have been told that they were beginning to grow the poppy largely in Victoria, and before long it will, depend upon it, be growing here. Prevention was better than cure the world over. Let us then, take up the matter seriously and earnestly; let us make our voices heard and in heaven's name stamp out the evil for ever while there was yet time." (Loud cheers.)

Quong Tart never lived to see the full glory of that day, when the efforts he had made found their fulfilment and embodiment in the conditions of the States, but we may safely say that in the high hours of vision he was permitted to see the dawn breaking on the not far distant hills, and he has gone down to history as a true herald of the dawn.

A Plea For The Abolition of the Importation of Opium.
By Quong Tart.

(The Profits of the Sale of this Pamphlet will be handed to the Committee for the Relief of the Sufferers by the recent Mining Disaster at Bulli.)

During the year 1884 a petition was presented to the Honourable the Executive Council of N.S.W. praying for the abolition of the importation of opium to this colony, except for strictly medicinal purposes; but the reception it met with was not nearly so favourable as was anticipated, notwithstanding the fact that the petition contained upwards of 4000 signatures of every nation and creed. No doubt 4000 is a small number compared with the whole population of the colony, but be it understood they consisted of the names of the principal clergy of every church, members of Parliament, nearly seventy mayors and aldermen, besides other leading residents of N.S.W., the Press, and over 500 Chinese.

Mr. Hardie, who was then Mayor of Sydney, and the Rev. Dr. Steel accompanied me when I presented the petition, in the presence of the Hon. G.R. Dibbs, to Sir. A. Stuart. Sir Alexander was quite in favour (as regards himself) of the abolition of the opium traffic, but he looked at it in this way — Were it not imported into this colony it would be smuggled into it from the various other colonies; subsequently, he said, "The smoking will not cease, but still the colony would lose the revenue, which is considerable." Our interview terminated by Sir A. Stuart promising to enter into communication with the adjoining colonies in order to ascertain whether they would do all in their power to suppress the trade. I fancy, however, that the other duties which our Parliament had to perform were regarded as of more importance and the opium question was forgotten, for nothing more has come of it, and the result of the action of those who interested themselves in the matter has been nil. I do not feel at all disheartened over that attempt, but intend to use all the personal influence I possess, and with the assistance of my friends make another attempt.

The Hon. G.R. Dibbs, assisted by Inspector Seymour and his officers, certainly deserve great praise for the manner in which they went with me to the various common Chinese places, to look into the condition of affairs for themselves. Some persons were caught indulging in the use of the juice, while others heard of the intended visit and were prepared. I really think that official visit in the city, Mr. Inspector Brennan's exertions in the country, and my own (the time I was sent by Inspector-General Fosbery to investigate the Chinese camps) frightened a number from commencing to smoke and restrained those who had just begun. But now, through the matter being allowed to lie in abeyance so long, they are, I am sure, as bad, if not worse, than before.

I wish to make it as clearly understood as possible that were a law to be passed against the importation of the juice, it would not only be an inestimable blessing bestowed upon the Chinese in general, but upon all classes of the community, for this drug, when indulged in by any person a few times, has such seductive qualities that it is almost an utter impossibility to keep it from him so long as money can procure it. It is not to be compared with intoxicating liquors, for people often turn against drink, but opium they never take a dislike to — not even in their dying moments; and the only way to prevent indulgence is to put it quite beyond the reach of those who have become slaves to it, and that can easily be done by allowing none but chemists to sell it, and then to those only who produce a note from a duly qualified medical practitioner. It may be mentioned that that sold by chemists is vastly different from that used by the Chinese — it undergoes a different preparation, and it would be of no use to them for smoking.

There would still be a slight revenue from opium, so that the Government would not lose all revenue derived from it. Then again, the Chinese who were in the habit of smoking it would smoke tobacco instead. and that would give an additional revenue in another direction. But I am sure none of the worthy gentlemen comprising our present Parliament would say "import opium for the sake of revenue," because such broad-minded and highly principled men as we have amongst our free-traders and protectionists would consider the saving of souls long before the question of £ s.d. I feel positive that there is not one gentlemen who would like to see anyone belonging to him using this slow poison, but if it is not stopped, they are sure, some of them, sooner or later, to be trapped. Then why should they not put themselves together as a body and stop it at once? Now is the time and the best time, while we have such a noble Governor as Lord Carrington, in the jubilee year of our most gracious Sovereign's reign. What more notable event could New South Wales do or have in this year than the "Abolition of Opium Importation"? I am sure every sensible and well-thinking man will say "None." I am almost certain that if New South Wales showed the example by stopping the traffic, Victoria would follow suit, judging from the way Mr. Service, who was then Premier, the Hon. Graham Berry, several members of Parliament, and the Inspector-General of Police treated me while I was trying to get an insight into the state of affairs as regards opium-smoking in that Colony. They took an active part with me in visiting some of the Chinese places in Melbourne. We were a little baffled in our first visit, but the second proved more successful, for we caught some (consisting of European women and Chinese) in the very act of smoking. The whole of the newspapers of that colony were in full favour of my exertions, as were also the leading Chinese merchants; and in Ballarat a meeting was held and everyone present supported the movement to stop the trade, and promised to do all that could be done to help me when called upon. That in itself speaks volumes.

When opium was first imported into China (by the East India Company), the authorities of that country did not see the evil, but as soon as they discovered it they tried to put a stop to it. Alas! it was too late, for they were prevented by international agreements, and all they could do was to shut their eyes and say no more. It is a most lamentable sight to view the misery existing in some of the habitations of China, caused simply by the use of opium. Homes that once were happiness itself, and supplied with every comfort, were denuded even of furniture of any description — all had been sold or disposed of by other means simply to gratify a taste for this cursed drug. I know of one case where the father of a family who used to be pretty well to do took to opium-smoking. His means ran short and he sold all he could, leaving the family quite destitute, to get money to buy opium. One of his sons became seriously ill and died. He had no means to bury him, and when he asked people for assistance he was refused, for no one in China will look upon or help an opium-smoker — no matter what his troubles may be. The mother, when things were in this terrible plight, gave him some money (she had saved by her own hard industry, unknown to him) to go and get their son a coffin. The father when he got the money, instead of putting it to the use intended, took it off to an opium house and smoked it all away. The mother anxiously waited for his return, but no. A messenger was despatched, who soon returned with the news that her husband was housed in an opium-shop, and had never been near the undertaker. This is only one case out of hundreds similar. Why not then try to stop it in this young country before it reaches a state equal to what I have described?

Evidences of the evils caused by opium-smoking were given me by Signor Raimondi, the Roman Catholic Bishop of Hongkong, during a conversation the other day. The Bishop had lived in China more than twenty-eight years, moving from one province to another, and he says it is totally impossible to describe the miseries the families of Chinese opium-smokers undergo. He goes further, and says he would not agree to opium being brought into this colony even for chemists except in a liquid condition. Any Chinaman known to use opium is not admitted to the Church. I think I can safely say that in twelve months' time after the prohibition of the importation, all gentlemen who have spoken publicly against the Chinese would speak very differently. Words cannot express how dreadfully hurt the respectable Chinese feel when things are said publicly against them, for the gentlemen who denounce make no allowance, but class all alike, although that is anything but fair, for no criminal case against the Chinese has ever come from any of the respectable business houses, large or small, but has in every case originated in places where opium is used. I had a conversation lately with some of the large Chinese importers, and they admit it is a cursed evil, and would be pleased to see it stopped from coming into the colonies. They said, "But as long as it is allowed to be imported, why should we not benefit as well as any other man." It is through this opium that the Chinese get indolent — in some cases too lazy or weak to keep their persons clean; that they crowd together in very badly ventilated rooms, where a number can, as they think, enjoy the poison together, and that horrible smell so many people complain of is caused. Then again — and worse than all — these men lose all inclination for work of any kind, and so commence that wicked and pernicious vice, gambling, simply because they can do it with little exercise of strength. I don't say for one moment that the police have not done their duty as far as hunting some of these gambling dens out, but I do say there are a number of places that are still to be found. Why not save the police this "blind man's buff" work by stopping the opium? Then the gambling would cease; and more than that, the Chinese, if they intend to remain in the colony, would completely reform with the assistance of the different Chinese clergymen (Church of England, Wesleyan, Presbyterian and Roman Catholic), and become more attached to the European customs, and in time form a splendid addition to the workers of this colony. Then some of the better class of people in China, when they find that the Chinese are being appreciated and held in a higher estimation by the people here, will cast in their lot amongst us. Whereas we have at present coming to the colony a very mixed class, for in numerous cases people are sent here by their relatives or parents because no good can be got out of them through their having taken to opium. I heard and saw (while on a visit to China in the year 1881) of some cases where the parents went so far as to threaten to murder their sons unless they gave up smoking opium, but even that did not frighten them — in fact, took no effect; so rather than see them go to ruin the parents gave them some money and sent them about their business. And where did they go? Well, to the place where they knew they could get any amount of opium without any remonstration from anyone.

At the time of the general outcry against the Chinese, the Government had a thorough investigation made of the Chinese camps in Wagga, Narandera, Deniliquin, Albury and Hay, in order to find out the cause, and it was the outcome of these men using opium. Not only the Chinese in these five places visited were found to use the drug, but also seventy-five European women, and out of the seventy-five fifty were confirmed smokers. Now, readers, you can imagine for yourselves the results, when so many were found in five places alone.

If the Government had stopped the importation then the cry would have ceased ere now, and as long as the use of opium is legalised, why cry out against the Chinese? Cry out rather against the Government for not stopping it, for the power is theirs and in their hands.

During my last attempt to get this curse removed, numberless squatters and other gentlemen wished me every success, for they have had in their employ Chinamen who smoke and those who do not. Speaking from experience, they said, "Get the traffic stopped for all that is good, because it is a cursed evil. I would sooner employ a drunkard any day than an opium-smoker." So, I pray that all will with one voice cry, "Stop the importation;" and if anyone be found after a certain date selling the opium, except chemists, let a very heavy fine be inflicted or a long term of imprisonment. The smuggling would be very slight, and could be easily detected — if by no other means, by the smell. The present large importers would have more honour than disgrace themselves by importing after the law was passed prohibiting its sale.

I wish all to understand that I have no other motive for taking up this great cause than true wishes and good feelings for the benefit and good of all, this generation and succeeding ones, living in New South Wales and even over the whole of Australia.

The following is a copy of a petition about to be presented to the Honourable the Speaker of the House of the Legislative Assembly of New South Wales:–

THE PETITION of the undersigned Citizens of the Colony of New South Wales, and also of Chinese Residents within the same:–

HUMBLY SHEWETH —

1. That your Petitioners, having in view the well-being of this community, regard with feelings of alarm, the increasing consumption of opium by Chinese residents of the colony.

2. That the use of opium is exceedingly hurtful to those persons who habitually indulge in that narcotic; and also to the general population, for the following reasons, namely:–

> (a) That the constant use of opium is calculated to impair the moral and physical systems and consequently to induce habits of indolence.
>
> (b) That by reason of the indolence so produced, persons are unfitted for and undesirous of pursuing any mechanical or other useful occupation; and to this cause are to be attributed the gambling and criminal propensities of those Chinese who consume opium.
>
> (c) That the conditions under which opium is consumed in this community cause large numbers of Chinese to assemble in ill-ventilated and crowded apartments, whereby, in addition to the essential evil arising from the use of opium, these resorts are turned into hotbeds for the generation of fevers and cognate diseases.
>
> (d) That many European girls and women, after being induced to use the narcotic, become habitues of the same resorts, and scenes of the grossest immorality ensue.

3. That your Petitioners desire to point out that the use of opium in China is confined to the very lowest orders of Chinese society, and that those using it are unfavourably regarded by their fellow-countrymen.

4. That in the event of the introduction of opium into New South Wales being prohibited by law, there will be very little inducement for its consumers to come to this colony; while on the other hand, Chinese of a superior class, recognising that under the altered conditions their presence on these shores will be more favourably regarded, will, in all probability, cast in their lot among us.

Your Petitioners, therefore humbly pray —

That at an early date a measure may be framed and laid before Parliament, prohibiting the importation of opium into this colony, excepting for medicinal purposes; and that such measure may also provide against the sale of opium excepting for medicinal purposes, and where the purchaser produces a satisfactory prescription or certificate from a duly and legally qualified medical practitioner requiring that the same may be supplied.

And furthermore that the said measure may be so framed as to come into operation at the expiration of six months from the passing thereof.

And your Petitioners, as in duty bound, will ever pray, &c., &c.

Dated at Sydney this fifth day of April, in the year of our Lord one thousand eight hundred and eighty-seven.

Quong Tart — Sportsman.

Quong Tart was a lover of sport. Not any kind of sport, but sport that was above all things clean. He looked upon horse-racing as a splendid pastime, and at one time owned a race-horse and was his own jockey. Braidwood people will remember his stirring rides in that district on his favourite horse "Nobby." He was an expert rider and prided himself on being able to keep his seat on a buckjumper.

But the advent of the gambling element resulted in his exit, for gambling was in his opinion an evil deserving of a place alongside of opium in its power to ruin home and destroy national life.

True sport, sport in which the chance element was at a minimum and skill at a maximum, always found in him an ardent supporter. In his quaint humorous way, and peculiar mixing of metaphor, he gave expression to the principles in the spirit of which he thought all games should be carried out. Addressing the League of Wheelmen, he said, "he hoped the members of the League would act honourably in their racing and have no shinaniking. If they raced right out from the shoulder they were bound to get on. The man who shinaniks is unworthy of the name of a British bicyclist."

In this and other ways he sought to elevate sport into a purer atmosphere than that which sometimes surrounded it, and in his speeches tried to impress upon sportsmen the necessity to preserve their prestige and integrity by going straight and doing their best to win.

He took a keen interest in cricket and while in the Braidwood district was one of the most enthusiastic cricketers. In many a match he was the hope of their "side," and by the scores he made proved conclusively that he certainly was.

On moving to Sydney he still continued to take an active part in cricket. On March 30th, 1898, a match between the Ladies and Theatricals — in aid of the Queen Victoria Hospital for Consumptives Fund — took place.

Later on at a social the ladies of the Novelty Cricket Match presented Mr. Tart with a large frame containing portraits of the lady cricketers, and the original rosettes worn by them on March 30th. Mr. Ironside, on behalf of Mrs. Capt. Donnan and the ladies of the team, made the presentation,

To explain the reason of the presentation it must be told that after the match, Mr. Tart expressed a wish to have a little piece of the rosette worn by each lady as a memento of the occasion, and thinking this request over, Mrs. Capt. Donnan came to the conclusion that it would be a graceful acknowledgment of the great kindness shown by Mr. Tart to give him the rosettes in their entirety — a unique gift, as the rosettes and their peculiar associations could not be duplicated or reproduced.

Still later he was elected Vice-President and Starter of the League of New South Wales Wheelmen.

He was much interested in football and lacrosse, and especially in the game of bowls, being a member for years of the City Club.

Hardly a week went by that he did not have at his rooms some "Sport" or "team of Sports," and sportsmen from other States and from all over the world were always sure in coming to New South Wales that there was one man who would extend genuine hospitality to them, and that man was Quong Tart.

List of Societies and Clubs he was a member of:–

Highland Society.
Royal Agricultural Society.
Zoological Society (life member).
Horticultural Society.
Society of Artists.
Camden Agricultural and Horticultural Industrial Society.
Hospital Saturday Fund.
Australian Ambulance Association (life governor).
Judge, A., P., H. and T. Association, Cootamundra.
Freemason Society.
City Night Refuge.
League of Wheelmen (Starter).
City Bowling Club.
Ashfield Bowling Club.
International Tug of War.
Burwood Cycling Club.
Summer Hill Owl Club.
Sydney Cricket Club.
Waverley Football Club.
Park Grove Football Club.
Sydney Flying Squadron.
Sydney Dinghy Sailing Club.
Johnstone's Bay Sailing Club.
City Band, Balmain Coldstream Band, also Ashfield Band.
N.S.W. League of Swimmers.

Quong Tart.

Things Humorous from Him and about Him.

Quong Tart was a happy man. He was one of those highly favoured individuals upon whom the sun of gladness seemed not to set. It mattered not where he might be — feasting the poor, speaking at a social gathering, or plunging into business — he, in all circumstances maintained a happy state of unruffled evenness. Men may come and men may go, but Mr. Tart's happiness seemed to flow on forever. He was a ready-witted, mirth-provoking companion, and had ingrained in his Anglicised Chinese composition a dash of the philosophical, which tended to make him an agreeable and valuable auxiliary to any society. Sparkling with fun, brimful of humour, Quong Tart created amusement wherever he went. His speeches on special occasions, his renderings of songs of all nationalities were always calculated to put people in a very happy frame of mind. Those who knew the little man, five feet five inches in height, will remember his irresistible smile and genius for seeing a joke and making one.

On one occasion, Lord Hampden was at the League Sports. His Excellency started the Ten Miles Scratch Race. Quong was the usual operator of the pistol for the League. In handing the weapon to his Excellency, he said: "You know, they would much rather see you start the race than me." "How is that?" queried Lord Hampden, with a smile. "Because," said Mr. Tart, with a very broad grin, "you're a big gun and I am only a little one."

At a banquet held in Sydney somebody pressed him to take more fizz, but as the amber fluid had been round more than once, the Mandarin refused, saying: "No, thanks. If I took more of that stuff, I shouldn't be a tart, but a rolypoly."

Mr. Hawthorne, ex-Member for Leichhardt, writes: "As intimate friend of Mr. Tart's and companion on many of his journeys, I was specially delighted with his ready wit. Out for a picnic he was always the life of the party, keeping it almost in a state of perpetual merriment. At special gatherings his speeches were unapproachable for the humour they displayed and the applause they always evoked. It was my privilege to be present with him at the opening of a Church Bazaar in Merewether on one occasion. During the evening one of the ladies at the stalls was boasting of the fowls and the eggs of the district. She had large eggs, eggs in any quantity, and double-yolked eggs. When Tart got up to speak he said: 'You good people pride yourselves on your goods, and one lady says she has the best eggs in the world in her stall, big eggs, double-yolked eggs, and that nothing can approach the eggs the hens of her district lay, but I tell you that's simply nothing. Here's Mr. Hawthorne, M.P. I was with him at Leichhardt last week, and his good wife — why, I saw her lay a foundation stone two ton weight!'"

On one occasion he was invited by Sir Wm. Lyne to accompany him and a number of other prominent citizens, including a good sprinkling of Members of Parliament to an excursion in the Government steamer, "Captain Cook," to Byron

Bay for the purpose of turning the first sod of the Casino to Lismore railway, and as he was not a good sailor some friends advised him to take a patent medicine to prevent sea-sickness. This he did, with the result for the whole of the journey he was huddled up on the deck of the steamer a most pitiable object. In addressing a public meeting afterwards in Lismore, he caused roars of laughter in relating the above circumstances, which he did in his own peculiar manner, and wound up a humorous speech by advising his hearers on no account to try and stop sea-sickness by any artificial means, or they would find out some day what he nearly found out, that the undertaker's services would be required at the first port of call.

At a tea-meeting at Ashfield after the Rev. Cakebread had spoken, Mr. Tart was asked to say a few words. "Friends," he began, "you have no taste for good things; you eat this cake and that cake until you're full; but the real Cakebread and the genuine Tart you leave untouched."

Speaking at the League of Wheelmen Meeting on one occasion he said: "What the Government wants is co'litions; what the bicycler wants is to keep off co'lisions."

In the singing of Scotch songs he delighted great audiences.

"At one time," says a writer, "I went to the Patti Concert with a resident of Randwick and her little girl. Among her many successes the 'diva' made a more than common one in 'Comin' Thro' the Rye," the business she introduced of nodding her head being particularly pretty and most effective. As we drove home, my friend said, 'Didn't Patti sing charmingly? Much better than she did at Monte Carlo. And wasn't it pretty in "Comin' Thro' the Rye" to see her nod her head? So cheeky.' Then up spake the little girl, 'O, mother, you should have heard Quong Tart sing it. I did, and he nodded his head too, like this, and said, "Comin' Thro' Randwick," ' at which the mother and I leaned back in the cab and laughed till we cried. 'He did,' said Nada, gravely. 'We went to the Asylum.' 'Before or after,' said I. 'Why, before,' said Nada, 'it was at the entertainment.'"

No Highland Gathering was complete without him, and Scotchmen claimed him as one of their own kith and kin. The following article in a daily newspaper of the time in which the writer seeks to make him out a brawny Scot is highly amusing:–

"Jock Maclardy" kens for a fac that Mr. Quong Tart is a Scotchman by kith and kin, on his faether's side at ony rate. He supposes his first forefather that went to China, may be after Culloden, was a M'Pherson or ane o' the ither clans, and as the Chinamen could no' pronounce his name they tried to call him Tartan aefter the kilt and plaid he wore. As they couldna manage the whole word Tartan, however, they cauld him by the first syllable "Tart" and sae the name has come doon ever since. Jock thinks he should now take his full name, and call himself Mr. Quong Tartan, as it ought to be.

He himself always claimed to be Scotch in instinct and sympathy, and delighted to be referred to as Mac Tart. He amused thousands during his life by his rendering of Scotch songs, always on the strict Q. T. as he would jocularly remark.

Coming back from a short visit to Canton, the moment he struck the soil at Circular Quay, he stamped and said: "Wahoo! My foot is on ma native heath once mo' and ma name's Quong Tart Mah Graigor, O!"

Perhaps his last public appearance was at a suburban Church Concert, where the renowned MacTart was programmed to sing two Scotch songs. At the first essay, he solemnly announced: "Mr. Chairman, Ladies and Gentleman, the gentleman who engaged me for this concert is not present. I must, therefore, ask for my fee before I sing or a guarantee that it will be paid before I leave. I never sing under fifty guineas." It took the audience a few seconds before they saw the twinkle in Quong's eye, and then they roared. They rewarded him by encoring each song until he was tired.

A Bega man tells a story against himself relative to Quong Tart. A good many years ago he held a Government position and one day Quong Tart called on him to transact some business, tendering his cheque, which he refused to take. Quong remonstrated with him, and the official used some very forcible language in reply. "All right," said Quong; "you will hear more about this." He did, and was fined two pounds at the next Police Court sitting.

The following story, published in the "Tumut Courier" of November 6th, 1887, humorously describes the position taken up by a man who "drew the colour line":–

"Our worthy citizen, Mr. Quong Tart, has had rather a peculiar experience of late. A few days ago there came a cable from England that our Gracious Queen desired to thank 'Sir' Tart (he ought to be a knight now) for the Jubilee Congratulatory Address forwarded by him from the Chinese residents of Sydney, and this so delighted the Annie Laurie warbler that he went round looking as pleased as a peacock with two tails. A day or two after this saw a different scene, however, for the Mayor of Tumut 'gif a barty' and 'Sir' Tart, being in town, was duly invited. A telegram from the seat of war next day informed the world that all had not gone as happily as the circumstances of the case demanded, for we read that 'Mr. Q. Tart was an invited guest at the Mayor's Ball, but a simple fool of some property here refused the Mayor's invitation, and went so far as to restrain his wife from attending simply because Q.T. was present.' Mr. Q.T. may be good enough for the Queen of England to communicate with, but it would seem he is not quite good enough for the elite of Tumut. China has not yet declared war against Tumut over the above incident, but relations between the two great powers are pretty considerably strained."

"Quong Tart in Bathurst. — Some of the ladies said he was too sweet for anything — a sweet Tart, in fact. Which reminds me that when Quong Tart first started business in the Royal Arcade, King Street, a lady stepped into his refreshment rooms and asked the proprietor himself for 'a cup of tea and a quong tart.' He corrected her and for once forgot to smile."

"Mr. Quong Tart never terms a man 'a bad egg,' as that is libellous. He says he is an egg that has been laid a long time."

"The inscrutable Quong Tart, who is a great Mandarin, says China is only a big boy yet, ignorant of her strength, but when she finds it, she will shoot straight from the shoulder, and knock her enemies into a cocked hat."

"Quong Tart, as is his custom, has been lavishing his hospitality on Commandant and Mrs. Booth. The Commandant thought Quong would make a splendid organising officer for the Chinese Salvation Army, and Mrs. Booth said that for her part she thought Quong would 'look beautiful in a red jersey,' and she longed to 'decorate him with one.'"

Quong Tart always gave of his best, but the best was not always appreciated, as the following amusing incident shows:–

"The young gentlemen attached to a certain Governor's retinue were tendering a complimentary entertainment to the ladies, so they engaged Quong Tart to do the catering to ensure the thing being done in style. The genial Quong, not wishing to trifle with his reputation, brewed the beverage that cheers from choicest 'Bud' something or other that cost 7/6 per pound. When tea came on, the guests sipped gingerly, and then began to look dubious, and finally their faces assumed a betrayed aspect. After a little muttering and an exchange of opinions, one of the committee of management went to Quong Tart and said: 'Look here, old chap, what the dickens do you mean by giving us slop water for tea? Be good enough to have the damned stuff removed, and have something drinkable substituted.' More in sorrow than in anger, Quong ordered his staff to use some of the 'one and threepenny' tea. This was accordingly done, and the Government House 'Connoisseurs' pronounced it 'excellent, old chappie.'"

The same sunny, cheerful countenance he wore right up to the last, and to him the lines of Kendall may well be applied —

> His mind was like a summer sky,
> He lived a life of beauty.
>
> To lift his brothers' thoughts above
> This earth, he used to labour;
> His heart was luminous with love,
> He didn't wound his neighbour.

Short Story.

"Buried Alive."
A Bulgo Tunnel Agony!
Written by Quong Tart.

Illawarra is a beautiful place, but it has to be reached and left — on the Sydney side — through tunnels. Well, on Wednesday afternoon last, the 22nd of this month, No. 1 Shift of the Tramway Association people had a picnic, and, of course, they went to the "Garden of New South Wales," which somebody said once, and everybody says now, is Illawarra. Stanwell Park was picked as the centre of attraction for the day, and to that spot about 600 or 700 men, women and children made their way in a long train provided for the purpose. Several invited guests were among the party, including your humble servant, who tells this story.

Off we went in grand glee from Sydney, and, passing the National Park, popped through tunnel after tunnel like hide-and-go-seek. The long Bulgo tunnel, which was the last, but not the least, seemed to give some idea of what an Illawarra coal-mine must be like, except that we could not see any black diamonds about. When the train shot out of the tunnel, the view was beautiful past description. There seemed to be sea and shore and islands and blue sky and many other lovely features enough to occupy the pencils of all the artists this colony can produce for the next thousand years.

The picnic was a grand affair, as all the tramway picnics are. Everybody enjoyed themselves, husbands and wives (real and intended), children, visitors and all. But it is not the picnic I intended to tell about, but one little experience never to be forgotten by those who had a taste of it.

Our train, of twelve or thirteen carriages, started on the return journey about a quarter past six o'clock in the evening, intending to cross the down Wollongong train at Sutherland. But, as said by the Scotch philosopher, "The best laid schemes of mice and men gang aft aglee;" and so it was with us. We all got into the train, and started cheering and singing and waving hats and handkerchiefs, as if the iron horse were going to fly to Sydney, instead of running along the rails in the usual way. By slow degrees we disappeared into the Bulgo tunnel, and very soon we found that our engine had an up-hill job of it. It seemed as if some earthquake or giant had lifted the other end of the tunnel since we had gone through it the other way. And not only that, but it looked as if, at the same time, it had been stretched, like a piece of indiarubber, to many times its ordinary length, which, according to the contractors' measure, I am told, was a mile all but fifty yards. Slower and slower moved the train, and darker and darker grew the tunnel. Even with all the windows shut, the carriages got full of smoke and steam. The engine snorted, and coughed, and puffed, and barked, and sneezed, as if it had an attack of spasms and cholera and whooping cough and la grippe all in one, with no doctor within fifty miles of the spot. When, with the smoke and steam and grit in the carriages, everybody had to sneeze too, as if they had got into a pepper storm in the dark. There we were, as if we were to be buried alive. Darkness all around us like the grave, and the engine playing the "Dead March" for our funeral to the slowest of dead march time. We could just tell the train was moving forward, and that was all. But, horror of horrors! it came to a standstill at last, without the end of the tunnel being reached, though we thought in our agony we had gone far enough to reach George's River. The engine seemed to be giving its dying gasps, with a quivering sensation that sent a death-like feeling through all the train. Children cried and screamed as well as they could in the smoky darkness; women swooned and fainted, and in every way it looked as if the whole lot of picnickers were going to be stifled and smoked into bacon, to say the least. But just when it appeared as if it were all over with us, our good engine-driver proved himself the right man in the right place. When he found he could not go forward, he made up his mind to go back, and backward he sent the whole train at express speed. In less time than it takes to tell it, the train backed out of the south end of the tunnel again, which seemed life from the dead to everybody. We then got water for the fainted ladies, and got them round by degrees, and soon all were breathing freely once more.

The train was next divided into two parts, and off the engine started with the first lot of carriages, which it reached Otford with all right. Leaving that lot on the double line at Otford, it went back for the second half. And it is said that the last shall be first; so it was the case there, for the last part of the train taken through the tunnel became the first, as we made the final start from Otford for Sydney, which we reached an hour late, but saying to ourselves, under the circumstances, "Better late than never."

Instead of us crossing the Wollongong train at Sutherland, that train had to wait for us first at Loftus and then at Sutherland a full hour. Of course, we were "blessed" by the people in the delayed train for keeping them waiting, but if they knew the fix we were in, and how much better off than us they were, they would have pitied us instead. But much better to be blamed innocently than to deserve blame, about a tunnel adventure or anything else.

Sydney, October 27th, 1890.

Complimentary Letters and Addresses Received By Him.

A.

60.

Council of Education Office,

Sydney.

11th September, 1877.

Sir, —

I am directed by the Council of Education to acquaint you that, in accordance with the provisions of Section 22 of the Public Schools Act, His Excellency the Governor, with the advice of the Executive Council, has appointed you to be a member of the Public School Board at Bell's Creek.

I have the honour to be, Sir,

Your most obedient servant,

GEORGE MILLER,

For Secretary.

To Mr. Quong Tart,
Public School Board,
Bell's Creek.

To Quong Tart, Esq., Bell's Creek, N.S.W.

Dear Sir,

We, the undersigned, hear with regret that you are about to leave this district, where you have resided for over twenty years, since your childhood.

We cannot allow the occasion to pass without expressing the great respect which we entertain for you, a respect which is shared by the people of the district generally, with whom, amongst all classes you have mixed in a friendly way and taken part with them in all matters of interest publicly and privately, in a manner which has reflected the highest credit upon you, and gained you a large number of personal friends, who will be sorry to lose you from amongst them.

It is a great satisfaction for them to know, however, that you are removing to another sphere in order to advance your position in life, and to one in which you will not be precluded from again visiting us in time to come, thus keeping alive amongst us many pleasant reminiscences of the past, in which you are intimately connected.

We remain, Dear Sir,

Yours faithfully,

W. C. FOX (Solicitor).

S. F. MACKENZIE, M.A.

ROND. HASSALL

H. P. WILSON

THOS. I. ROBERTS
J. F. FLASHMAN
J. KEEGAN (Inspector of Police).
FRANK MASON, J.P.
JOHN FRASER
ALFRED McFARLAND (District Court Judge).
W. H. JOHNSON
JAS. BRUM, J.P.
JOHN KINGSLAND
JAS. ALDCORN (P.M., Araluen).
JOHN ROGERS
JAS LARMER, J.P.
CHAS. E. DRANSFIELD
W. M. V. TARPE, J.P.
JAS. McDONALD
JOHN H. BLATCHFORD, J.P.
JOHN MUSGRAVE
THOS. STEWARD, J.P.
THOS. FORSYTH
W. F. ROBERTSON, C.P.S.
CHRIS. C. ROBINSON
THOS. ACHINTON, J.P.

Braidwood, March, 1881.

I.O.O.F.M.U., N.S. Wales.
  Loyal Miners' Refuge Lodge, No. 73.
    Quong Tart.
Dear Sir and Brother,
We, the undersigned Committee of the above-named Lodge, respectfully request your acceptance of this Address, in testimony of the respect and esteem in which you are held by the brothers.

You were admitted a member of our Order in 1871, and have since been a contributive member without interruption, and whenever any occasion required, have with greatest urbanity and liberality given your personal and pecuniary assistance.

Wishing you may enjoy a long, useful and successful life, we subscribe ourselves, on behalf of this Lodge,
            Yours in Friendship, Love and Truth,
  JOHN ELLIS. P.P.G.M.
  WILLIAM DOUGLAS, P.G.
  HENRY BAUMGARDNER, P.G.
  MCHL. MADIGAN, P.N.G.
  WM. WALSHAM, Secretary.

Presented at Public Banquet on Wednesday, 16th March, 1881, at Major's Creek.

Wm. WALSHAM,
Chairman.

We, the Undersigned,

Having been informed that **Mr. Quong Tart** is about to proceed to China, with a view of establishing commercial relations with mercantile firms, **Hereby Testify** that our knowledge of him enables us to state that during a residence of twenty years in this Colony he has, by his strict integrity, unwearied perseverance, affability and genial conduct won the esteem and respect of all classes.

There is no man of any nationality more respected in the district in which he resided.

Signed at Sydney this fourth day of April, 1881.

JOHN ROBERTSON, K.C.M.G. ("Clovelly," Watson's Bay, late Premier).

HENRY CLARKE, M.P. (Victoria Wharf).

ALEXANDER STUART, M.P. (Sydney, of the firm of R. Evans and Co., late Treasurer).

HENRY MACREADIE (Presbyterian Minister, Sydney, the Very Reverend Moderator of Presbyterian Church).

JAMES S. FARNELL, M.P. (Sydney, New South Wales, late Premier).

JOHN MACINTOSH, J.P. (307 Pitt-street, Sydney).

EDWD. GREVILLE, J.P. (Late Member for Braidwood District).

WILLIAM MARKE, M.P. (Sydney).

R. L. MURRAY, M.P. (Sydney, New South Wales).

HENRY S. BADGERY, M.P. (Talwong, Summer Hill).

J. H. YOUNG, M.P. (Sydney, New South Wales).

WM. KELYNACK, D.D. (Ex-President Wesleyan Church, N.S.W.).

PHILLIP G. MYERS (Goulburn).

G. B. SIMPSON, J.P. (Barrister-at-Law, Sydney).

SYDNEY A. WANT (Sydney). (Solicitors, Sydney).

WM. CURTIS (Solicitor, Sydney).

J. H. WANT (Barrister-at-Law, "Clanie," Darling Point).

SULLIVAN & SIMPSON (Stock and Station Agents, 382 George-street, Sydney).

Department of Government Asylums for the
Infirm and Destitute.

Manager's Office,
Sydney, 1st Sept., 1886.

Dear Sir,

As Manager of the Government Asylums for the Infirm and Destitute, and on behalf of the Inmates of the Liverpool and Parramatta Institutions, I desire to thank you, and through you all who so warmly responded to your suggestion and so kindly aided you for the great treat you afforded these poor people, and I assure that one and all most gratefully appreciate the interest shewn in them.

Amongst the 1,500 inmates under my care at Liverpool and Parramatta, there are some who have seen "better days," and there are none who are not fully sensible of the kindness which prompted you to get up the late entertainment for them.

It has been very cheering and pleasant to hear the inmates talk of their treat, a bright day in their memories, and more than all, they are grateful for the thoughtfulness of their desolation and the efforts made to ameliorate their condition.

I am, Dear Sir,

Yours faithfully,

Frederic King,

Manager Asylums.

Mr. Quong Tart.

Dear Sir,

Having been informed that you purpose revisiting your native country, we desire that you should carry with you an expression of the estimation and respect in which you are held by those among whom you have lived.

It has been our opportunity, as representatives of the various sections of the people, to observe your life in its social, moral, and political aspects, and in each phase you have gained the warm approval of those among whom you resided. In the early days, when disputes were numerous relative to mining claims between Chinese and Europeans on the goldfields; you were generally called upon to act as sole arbitrator, and your decisions were always received by both parties as equitable.

You have acted as Interpreter in many very important cases, and your performance of the duty invariably gave satisfaction.

You depart from us bearing the esteem and goodwill of the whole community.

We venture to express the hope that your visit to China may be a means of softening recent asperities, and that you may be spared to return to our Colony, and to your wife and child, whose safety will be in our keeping, to renew a life of honour, health, and happiness amongst us.

Alfred Stephen,

G.C.M.G., C.B., Lieut. Governor of New South Wales.

W. C. WINDEYER (Judge of the Supreme Court of N.S.W.).

CHAS. L. GARLAND (M.L.A.).

M. H. STEPHEN (Judge of the Supreme Court of N.S.W.).

S. D. LANGLEY (Minister, Church of England, Sydney).

JOHN HAY, K.C.M.G. (President of the Legislative Council of New South Wales).

WM. KELYNACK (Minister).

GEO. H. COX (M.L.C.).

HARMAN J. TARRANT (M.R.C.S.E., Surgeon).

EDW. S. KNOX (M.L.C.).

J. CURRIE ELLES

ANDREW GARRAN, LL.D. (M.L.C.).

THOMAS E. DICKSON (Mayor of Waverley).

RICHARD HILL (M.L.C.).

JOHN MACPHERSON, J.P. (Alderman, Waverley).

JNO. M. CREED (M.L.C.).

E. P. SIMPSON, Q.C. (Attorney-General).

ARCHD. H. LACOL (M.L.C.).

SYDNEY A. WANT, Q.C. (Barrister)

SAMUEL CHARLES (M.L.C.).

BURTON BRADLEY (Solicitor).

GEO. THORNTON (M.L.C.).

STEPHEN, JAQUES, STEPHEN (Solicitors).

R. E. O'CONNOR (M.L.C.).

A. E. JAQUES (Solicitor).

JOHN MACINTOSH (M.L.C.).

EDWARD GREVILLE. J.P. (Journalist).

HENRY MOORE (M.L.C.).

GEO. ROBINSON (Journalist).

GEO. A. LLOYD (M.L.C.).

JOHN ROBERTSON (K.C.M.G.).

JOHN LACKEY (M.L.C.).

JOHN J. CALVERT (Clerk of the Parliaments).

GEO. R. DIBBS (M.L.A.).

ROBERT GUY, J.P. (Merchant).

JAMES FLETCHER (M.L.A.).

ALF. W. MEEKS (Merchant).

JOHN GALE (M.L.A.).

HENRY S. BADGERY (Merchant).

J. P. ABBOTT (M.L.A.).

EDWARD LLOYD JONES (Merchant).
A. J. RILEY (M.L.A.).
JOHN GRAHAM, J.P. (Merchant).
HUGH TAYLOR (M.L.A.).
H. FORSYTH (Merchant).
W. McMILLAN (M.L.A.).
A. L. NELSON, J.P. (Merchant).
JOHN SEE (M.L.A.).
A. C. HEWLETT, J.P. (Merchant).
E. W. O'SULLIVAN (M.L.A.).
E. JOHN FOX, J.P. (Merchant).
H. M. SLATTERY (M.L.A.).
W. BEAUMONT, J.P. (Merchant).
JULES JOUBERT (Exhibitions). Sydney, 8th November, 1888.

Sydney, N.S.W.,
June 28/'87.

To Quong Tart, Esq.
Dear Sir,

We, the undersigned employees of the Tramway Department, and lately members of the Committee of the Fancy Fair (of which you were one of the promoters) held at the Exhibition Building, April 22nd and 23rd, in aid of the widows, orphans and sufferers left by the disastrous explosion of the Bulli Colliery, would ask your acceptance of the accompanying photograph as a memento of that occasion, and also as a slight token of the regard and esteem we have for you as a true and valued friend.

We trust that you will ever enjoy true happiness, and that prosperity may always be your lot is the very earnest and heartfelt wish of yours faithfully and sincerely,

HUBERT JESSOP
JOHN SMITH
GEORGE GAMGEE.
JOHN HOLLINGWORTH.
WM. NOYCE
CHARLES SANTER
JAMES T. ENTWISTLE.

28 — 6 — '87.

Colonial Secretary's Office,
Sydney, 7th November, 1888.

This will introduce to you Mr. Quong Tart, a Chinese merchant of this city. Mr. Quong Tart has been a resident in this Colony for many years, and was instrumental in suppressing in a large degree the opium traffic amongst his countrymen in the Australian Colonies. He is a person generally respected and esteemed by all classes. He proceeds to Hong Kong on a pleasure trip, and I should be glad if any attention or assistance can be rendered to him during his travels.

> HENRY PARKES,
> Colonial Secretary.

Sydney,
7th November, 1888.
To Quong Tart, Esq.
Dear Sir, —

As you are about to leave us for a few months, on a visit to China, we, your employees in the office, tea rooms, &c., &c., desire to take the opportunity of expressing our very great thankfulness for all your many kindnesses to us, for the deep interest you have always taken in our welfare, and your constant concern for our comfort.

We sincerely hope that you may have a safe and pleasant voyage to your native land, find all your relations well, receive a warm and hearty welcome from your countrymen, whom you have done so much for, that your visit may in every way be satisfactory, and that you may be brought back again safely to your dear ones here.

Wishing long life and happiness to Mrs. Tart, your dear daughter, and self, and hoping that you will accept this address as a humble testimony to our esteem and affection.

> We are, Sir,
> Yours sincerely,

JOHANNA STALKER
ANNIE TUCKER
ELLEN GOLDSTONE
C. A. LOOK
M. A. FRASER
THOMAS KEIR
MAY FORD
M. M. PRIESTLEY
CHARLES G. HOBBES
LIZZIE GLANVILLE
OLIVE YATES
M. JESSEP
MARTHA FROST
E. BROADLEY
M. MATHIESON
W. WATSFORD
L. BUSH
ERNEST E. FOUNTAIN

Lewington House,
Milson's Point, St. Leonards,
3rd November, 1888.

Quong Tart, Esq.

My Dear Sir,

I send you a testimonial, which you may shew to Missionaries and others in the cities of China which you may visit. You will especially find Presbyterian Missionaries from America in Canton, and from England and Scotland in Amoy and Swatow.

I hope your visit may prove useful to the Chinese, and beneficial to yourself.

Owing to my visit to Melbourne, I am unable to take any part in the public expression of esteem, but I am happy to send this written expression of my regard for you personally, and my confidence in all your benevolent efforts.

I am,

Yours sincerely,
ROBERT STEELE.

COPY OF TESTIMONIAL.
To Presbyterian Missionaries and Others in China.

This is to certify that I have known the bearer, Mr. Quong Tart, a Chinese Merchant in the City of Sydney, New South Wales, for a number of years, and have pleasure in stating that he has maintained a good reputation as a citizen, a merchant and a philanthropist; that he has been distinguished for his charitable works among the poor and his hospitality to all engaged in good work; that he has taken an intelligent and sympathetic interest in the conditions of the Chinese in Australia, by earnest efforts to get the sale of opium to them prohibited by law, in which he has been supported by many; that he has done much to promote pacific relations between Europeans and Chinese, and during recent agitations proved very useful; that he now visits China with a view to allay irritation among the Chinese, and to explain how matters stand in relation to the Chinese in these Colonies; that he has shown a sympathy with Christian work; and finally, that he is commended to the confidence of Missionaries and others whom he may meet in China.

ROBERT STEELE, D.D.,
Minister of St. Stephen's Presbyterian Church.

Sydney, New South Wales,
3rd November, 1888.

LETTER OF INTRODUCTION.

Newington College,
Stanmore,
November 6th, 1888.

To the Superintendent,
Wesleyan Mission,
Canton.

My Dear Brother,

I send this letter to introduce to you Mr. Quong Tart, a Chinese gentleman who has been for many years a resident in the Colony of New South Wales. During several years he has been carrying on the business of a tea merchant in Sydney, where he has won the highest esteem of all who have the pleasure of his acquaintance.

His manliness and integrity, his keen interest in social questions, notably among which I might name the labour he has put forth in seeking to abate the evils of opium-smoking, and the hearty good-will with which he has sought to brighten the lot of both old and young who are inmates of State Asylums, his active and untiring zeal to forward the best interests of his fellow-countrymen during a time of agitation and excitement, these are qualities which have deservedly secured him the esteem of all classes.

I have known him as a friend for a long time, and he has been a frequent visitor to my house and family. It is with much pleasure that I write this note introducing Mr. Tart to your notice. I may add that in thus writing I give expression not only to my own sentiments, but also to the sentiments of many others both among our ministers and people.

Wishing you much success in your great work,
I am,
Yours in fraternal regards,
WM. KELYNACK,
President of Newington College.
Ex-President of N.S.W. Annual Conference.

Centenary Hall,
Sydney,
May 22nd, 1890.

Quong Tart, Esq.
Dear Sir,

I have very much pleasure in conveying to you the cordial thanks of the Wesleyan General Conference, which was expressed by a formal resolution, for your kind hospitality, and the opportunity afforded the Conference for a pleasant gathering at your rooms on the evening of Tuesday, May 20th.

I have the honour to be,
Yours sincerely,
H. T. BURGESS,
Secretary of the Conference.

Colonial Secretary's Office,
Sydney,
20th August, 1891.

Sir,

I am directed by the Colonial Secretary to inform you that His Excellency the Governor, with the advice of the Executive Council, has been pleased to appoint you, in conjunction with the other gentlemen as named below, to be a member of a Royal Commission to make a diligent and full inquiry with the view of ascertaining the undoubted facts in the matter of alleged illicit gambling and immoralities among the Chinese resident in George Street North in the City of Sydney and neighbourhood, and the alleged bribery or misconduct of any members of the Police Force in relation thereto; also to make visits of inspection to localities in the said City and Suburbs occupied by Chinese, and investigate and report upon social conditions, means of sanitary provision in the dwellings and workshops, the callings or occupations and other circumstances affecting the well-being of such persons.

2. The Commission, which bears this day's date, has, I am desired to add, been forwarded to the President.

I have the honour to be,
Sir,
Your most obedient servant,
CRITCHETT WALKER,
Principal Under-Secretary.

Quong Tart, Esq.,
King Street,
Sydney.

The Right Worshipful,
William Patrick Manning, Esq., J.P.,
Mayor of Sydney,
President,
Francis Abigail, Esq., J.P.
John Stuart Hawthorne, Esq.,
and
Ramsay McKillop, Esq.

Oddfellows' Offices,
M.U. Hall,
Elizabeth Street,
Sydney,
25th April, 1892.

Dear Sir and Brother,

The Officers of the above Order desire to convey to you, on behalf of the

Manchester Unity in New South Wales, their best thanks for the kind, generous and brotherly manner in which you entertained the Officers and Deputies attending the Grand Annual Committee of 1892.

I am,

Yours faithfully,
EDWIN SCHOFIELD,
Grand Sec.

Brother Quong Tart,
   King Street,
      Sydney.

To QUONG TART, Esq.

Sydney, 17th April, 1894.

Dear Sir,

On the occasion of your leaving Sydney for a short visit to China, we, the undersigned, representing the Church of England Chinese Mission in this city, desire to express our regard and esteem for you as a citizen, and our appreciation of your unvarying interest in the moral and spiritual good of your fellow-countrymen.

We gratefully acknowledge our indebtedness to you for much counsel and advice in connection with the Mission, especially in its early history; and we believe that you rejoice with us over its growth and development.

We trust that with God's blessing, the new Chinese Church, respecting which you have shown such a deep interest, may ere long be commenced, and that on your return to Sydney you may see it completed.

Your unceasing labour, often almost single-handed, to put a stop to the indiscriminate sale of opium in this colony is now being taken up by a large and representative committee of the citizens, and we feel sure that it will in due season be crowned with success.

Wishing you, Mrs. Quong Tart, and your family a pleasant and prosperous journey, and a safe return to the Colony,

We are, your sincere friends,

WILLIAM M. COWPER,
   Administrator of the Diocese of Sydney in the absence of the Lord Bishop.

S. D. LANGLEY,
   Superintendent, Chinese Mission.

W. A. CHARLTON,
   Hon. Sec., Sydney Chinese Mission.

E. P. FIELD,
   67 Elizabeth Street.

GEORGE SOO HOO TEN.

JAMES WING.
TIMOTHY JOY CHEW.
PETER SHOO.

To Quong Tart, Esq., of Sydney

Dear Sir, —

As you are about to depart on a prolonged visit to China, we desire, on behalf of the whole of your employees, to give expression to the feelings of high esteem which we bear towards you.

Many of us have been in your employment for a number of years, and we gladly acknowledge your constant interest in our welfare, your uniform kindness, and your frequent acts of generosity towards us.

Sincerely and with respect do we say that we have found in you not only an employer, but also a friend; and the friendly feelings that have at all times existed have caused us to feel a pleasure in the performance of all our duties.

We congratulate you on the high position of respect and influence to which you have attained both in Sydney and throughout New South Wales, and we, who by our daily duties are brought into such close relationship to you, say, with all our hearts, that the praise and honour which have been so abundantly conferred upon you by the press and by prominent public men have been richly deserved.

We feel confident that you need no assurance from us that we will be loyal to your interests in your absence.

It is our earnest wish that Mrs. Tart, yourself, and family may have a pleasant voyage, an enjoyable holiday, and a safe return. We wish you farewell, and bid you God-speed.

> We remain, Dear Sir,
> > Yours respectfully,

ALFRED B. HOOPER,

General Manager, on behalf of Male Employees.

M. G. REDFORD,

Manageress, on behalf of Female Employees.

W. H. FARR,

On behalf of Kitchen Staff.

20th April, 1894.

To WHOM IT MAY CONCERN.

This will serve to introduce Mr. Quong Tart, of this City — a Chinese merchant in extensive business.

During the many years of my official life as Head of successive Administrations, I have had many opportunities of observing Mr. Tart's conduct which has been uniformly such as to secure to him the respect of his fellow citizens. He has established a character for energy and integrity, and has at all times largely and liberally joined in the charities of the community.

Mr. Quong Tart is married to an English lady, and has a small family.

HENRY PARKES.

Sydney,
New South Wales,
March 1st, 1894.

LETTER OF INTRODUCTION.

Government House,
   Sydney,
      April 13th, 1894.

Dear Sir,

Mr. Quong Tart, a naturalised citizen of this Colony, is about to visit his native country for the purpose of facilitating commercial relations between Sydney and the principal Chinese Ports.

Apart from the estimation Mr. Quong Tart is held in by the commercial world, he is highly and justly esteemed here for the energetic manner in which he has supported all philanthropic movements. I shall be grateful for any assistance you may be able to afford him.

I have the honour to be,
Yours faithfully,

R. W. DUFF.

To His Excellency,
  Sir W. Robinson, K.C.M.G.,
    Hong Kong.

New South Wales,
Chief Secretary's Office,
Sydney,
18th April, 1894.

This will introduce Mr. Quong Tart, Mandarin of the Chinese Empire, and a naturalised citizen of this colony.

Mr. Tart has been resident in New South Wales now for very many years, and is held in the highest esteem by all classes of the community.

He is proceeding to China for business purposes, and any attention or information that may be afforded him will be regarded as a favour by this Government.

GEORGE R. DIBBS,
Chief Secretary of New South Wales.

Lodge of Tranquility, No. 42,
United Grand Lodge of N.S.W.,

Sydney, N.S.W.,
18th April, 1894.

Dear Brother Quong Tart,

On your departure for China, we feel that we cannot let you go without expressing to you our hearty good wishes for a pleasant voyage and a safe return; your career amongst us, not only as a Mason, but as a good citizen, has won and maintained our esteem, and especially do we value your noble efforts in the various philanthropic movements in which you have actively engaged yourself.

Commending you to the brethren in China, praying that the G. A. O. T. U. may pour down His blessing upon you, and wishing you and Mrs. Tart and the children health and happiness,

We are,
Yours fraternally,

J. D. WARD, W.M.
T. AYERS, J.W.
J. HERMAN, S.W.
LEWIS SAMUELS, S.W.

Railways, New South Wales,

Ashfield,
20th April, 1894.

Quong Tart, Esq.,
Sydney.

Dear Sir,

On the eve of your departure for China, we, on behalf of ourselves and many other prominent officers and employees of the New South Wales Railways, beg to convey to you our respect and esteem in return for the valuable aid and kindness rendered to us at all times, and wish you, your good wife and family a safe and most pleasant voyage and speedy return.

We, with great respect and kind regards, beg to subscribe ourselves,

Yours very faithfully,

MOSS BROWNE, Station Master.
E. R. WILLIAMS, R. Station Master.
WILLIAM FINLAY, Chief Booking Clerk.
WILLIAM MONTGOMERY, Employee, G.R.
JAMES C. LEWIS, Employee
SIDNEY HULL, Goods Clerk.
ROBERT HENLEY, Employee.
J. HOOPER, Clerk.
W. WHITE, Guard, N.S.W.
M. A. L. de PLATER, Signalman

H. LAMBERT, Guard.
G. P. DAVIES, Porter.
GEORGE COURTMAN, Shunter.
JOSEPH HARRISON, Guard.
GEORGE PICKLES, Fettler.
ROBERT DEWS, Ganger.
LAWRENCE McSULLEA, Guard.
JOHN REILLY, Guard.
PETER P. MONJON, Ticket Collector.
W. CLISSOLD, Guard.
A. G. LEE, Guard, N.S.W.R.
G. MINTO, Guard.
JAMES GALATHORP, Guard, N.S.W.R.
J. BLINKINSOPP, Employee, N.S.W.R.
RICHARD COX, Guard.

Extract from "Sydney Daily Telegraph," 28th January, 1896:–

"Accident to Mr. Quong Tart. — Mr. Quong Tart met with an accident at his residence, Ashfield, yesterday morning. Mr. Tart was descending the stairs with a child on his shoulder, and in attempting to save the child, which had over-balanced itself, Mr. Tart missed his footing and fell to the bottom of the stairs. Dr. Collingwood was at once sent for. It was found that Mr. Tart had fractured one of his ribs."

Through the accident, Quong Tart was absent from Sydney for a couple of weeks, during which time he received many letters of sympathy — a copy of one reads:–

Ashfield G.R.

Memorandum to —
    Quong Tart, Esq.,
        "Gallop House,"
            Ashfield.
Dear Sir,
It may be pleasing to you to know amongst your innumerable friends in the Colony, there are the railway folk, who are deeply interested in your present misfortune, particularly so, nearly, if not all, the guards and employees on the Suburban Line, but especially those at the "Ashfield Station," who wish to convey to you their deepest sympathy, and trust you may soon be able to get about and better than ever. With every respect to your esteemed self, Mrs. Tart and family, trusting that you may be spared for many years yet to come,
    Yours very faithfully,
      E. R. WILLIAMS.
      WM. KEATING.

M. S. BROWNE, S.M.
M. DE PLATER.
WM. FINLAY.
WM. BOYLE.
G. COURTMAN.
A. BUMFORD.
A. DUCKETT.
ADAM PLATT.
F. RIMM.
JNO. HOOPER.
JAS. S. WHITE.
J. D. EDMONDS.
JOHN WILSON.
                    On behalf of all the other staff, etc.,

                    Secretaries' Office,
                          84 Elizabeth St., Sydney,
                              3rd November, 1902.

Quong Tart, Esq.,
   George Street.
Dear Sir,
On behalf of the Committee of the Orphans' Fair, we have to tender to you
their thanks for the great kindness you showed us in organising the now
memorable Chinese "Tug of War" at the Town Hall during the Fair. All those
who saw the spectacle warmly praised it. We may safely say that it was one of
the great draws of the Bazaar.
   Again thanking you for your kindness.
                          Yours faithfully,
                          HENRY G. QUIGLAN
                          C. G. HEPBURN
                                 Hon. Secs.,

His lady sympathisers were very numerous. The following lines were received at
the time from the Lady Superintendent of Flower Missions:–

                    World's Women's Christian Temperance Union.
                          Flower Missions Department
                          Newtown, New South Wales, Australia.

   Cheer up, old friend! The heat is trying,
      And broken ribs are trying, too;
   But a broken heart is worse than either,
      And this can ne'er be felt by you.

Your wife is worth her weight in diamonds,
    Your children dear as dear can be;
Your friends are counted by the million,
    And send their love to poor Q. T.

And hope that he may soon be better,
    And take his place in town again;
As nimble and as bright as ever,
    Without a care or twinge or pain.

So do not fret and make it longer,
    Before your kindly face we see,
Whene'er we call at the rooms in King Street
    To get a scone and a cup of tea.

But just be patient, do not worry,
    But be as good as good can be;
And you'll get well in half a jiffy;
    Just try it, like our good Q. T.

Please give my love to your good lady
    (I hope she will not jealous be),
And for yourself take a very large portion
    From yours mostly truly —

                        A. J P
January 28th, 1896.

The Story of the Assault.

It is indeed mysterious that one so popular with his fellows as Quong Tart was, should be the victim of an assault which nearly cost him his life. But such was the case.

At a quarter-past eleven on the morning of August 19th, 1902, while seated in his office, an unknown man entered and struck him on the head several times with an iron bar.

The circumstances of the case were startling in their audacity and simplicity. The office in which the assault was committed was on the same floor of the Queen Victoria Markets as his Elite Hall, but some distance away, and on the other side of the landing. It consisted of two connected departments. The door of the outer one opened on the inside balcony of the Markets, and the window of the inner one overlooked George Street. The inner room was used by Mr. Tart as his office and contained his safe, account books and confidential papers. The outer room contained piled up chests of tea, all but a passage to the inner office, being used in this way.

It appeared that the assailant first waited on him on the previous Monday morning. He stated that he had some tea to dispose of. Mr. Tart was not anxious to do business with one whose appearances gave little indications of a reliable connection, and he told the man he was too busy to see him. At this the man went away, presumably because the opportunity necessary for his purpose was not sufficiently favourable.

On the morning of the 19th, at ten minutes past eleven he again presented himself at the office. Mr. Tart was engaged with one of his employees, and the man went away. Apparently he did not go far, but waited until the employee left the office. When Mr. Tart was alone he walked into the office and began an extraordinary story. He said he was a detective, and had come to inform him that it had come to the ears of the police that there was a plan on foot to rob him. As a detective he had been told off to watch the premises. He stated that the robbery would be attempted by one of the Redfern Murderers. Such a story considerably alarmed its hearer. Nevertheless, he was by no means satisfied as to its authenticity. He was well acquainted with most of the officers of the detective department and the man before him was an entire stranger. Neither did his appearance nor manner suggest the detective. He had a handkerchief under his chin, partly covering his face and knotted under a black hat.

In answer to a question of his genuineness the stranger stated that his name was Smith, and that he had but recently joined the detective staff. He accounted for his dress and the handkerchief by saying he was disguised, and he recalled to Mr. Tart that he was the same man who had waited on him the day before regarding the sale of some tea. He then suggested that he should ring up the detective office on the telephone and inquire as to his statements. Mr. Tart was far from satisfied, turned to the telephone on his table that communicated with the clerk's office. He had turned the handle, and was picking up the receiver when the man struck him violently over the head with an iron bar.

The weapon was about eighteen inches long and had been held hidden inside his coat. A piece of newspaper had been pasted round it, doubtless with a view of allaying suspicion should it be seen. At the first blow Mr. Tart was knocked backwards over his chair. The assailant made several other blows at him, but the victim received them on his hands, which he had raised to protect himself. Warning the injured man to keep quiet, the assailant snatched up the money on the table, amounting to about twenty pounds and which Mr. Tart had been intending to bank. Three cheques that were also lying near he did not touch. He passed out of the office and made his way down the stairs into George Street.

Bleeding profusely, and almost stunned, Mr. Tart left his office and went to the Elite Hall. He gave instructions that a doctor should be summoned and the police informed. Dr. Robert Wilson was telephoned for, but in the meantime Sergeant Irwin, of the Glebe Police Station, rendered first aid. On arrival, the doctor dressed the injuries. It was found that Mr. Tart was suffering from a contused wound in the head and injuries to both hands.

Mrs. Tart was informed, and had her husband conveyed to their home in Ashfield. Superintendent Potter and Detective Bradley arrived on the scene in haste. They went closely into the case, and as a result of their enquiries were hopeful of quickly effecting an arrest.

The news of the assault quickly spread through the City, and during the afternoon hundreds of persons including a great number of the most prominent business men in the City, called at Mr. Tart's office to express their sympathy. Telegrams and letters came from all over the country, expressive of sorrow for what had happened.

As soon as he was able, Mr. Tart described the encounter in his own graphic way.

"I was in my office, sitting at my desk," he explained, "when this man came in. He came in and half closed the door. Then when I asked him what he wanted, he said, 'I'm a detective.'"

"I didn't like the look of him. When he said he was a detective, I asked him again what he wanted and he said that he came to warn me; to tell me that some thieves were going to make an attack upon me."

"Then I said: 'Well, if you are a detective, I don't know you. I know all the detectives.' He answered by saying: 'Oh, but I am a new man.' He went on to say that if I did not believe him I could telephone to the office and find out for myself. I asked him: 'What is the number of the Detective Office?' He hesitated, and I said 'Oh it's all right.'"

"I could see the fellow was up to no good by the suspicious way in which he was going on, so I thought I would ring up one of my clerks and ask him to come upstairs. I thought it would be better to have some assistance at hand in case he tried to do anything; for my office is a quiet place, and when you are inside you could kick up a great row, and probably nobody would hear you outside."

"As I turned the handle of the telephone and took up the receiver, the fellow closed the door more, and took a step towards to where I was sitting at the desk. He said, 'Here I will show you how to do it.' At the same instant he pulled something out, which he had either been carrying hidden under his arm or which he had under his coat. It looked like a piece of stick wrapped in newspaper, but I think it was a bar of iron by the weight of it. It was about a foot and a half long."

"Almost before I knew that he had it in his hand, he had hit me over the head with it. I sang out, 'Here, what are you doing?' and I jumped up at him, but he hit me quickly three or four times over the head again. I thought I was killed. I said: 'For God's sake don't kill me. What do you want to kill me for? If you want the money that is no reason why you should kill me."

"He gave another blow at my head, but I raised my hand to protect myself."

"Then he swept the money off the table into his pocket, and ran away. As he was taking the money and I was struggling to get up, he said 'Don't you try to follow me or I will kill you.' He ran out of the office and slammed the door."

The appearance of the office when visited soon after the perpetration of the robbery was eloquent confirmation of Mr. Tart's graphic story. Everything was in confusion. Papers from the opened table-desk were scattered all over the floor. The office chair on which he had been sitting was overturned beside an open iron safe filled with papers and account books. Though the safe door was pushed right back, there was no sign that the safe had even been looked into. How profusely Mr. Tart's wounds had bled was evident from the amount of blood which was about the office. Chairs, desk, papers and the floor were as though a murder had been committed; there were the same red fluid everywhere, plentifully besprinkled.

The police were for some time baffled in their attempts to secure the arrest of the assailant, but after several weeks the extreme cleverness of Sub-Inspector Roche and Senior-Sergeant M'Lean, assisted by Senior-Constable Macintosh and Constables Clarke and Coombes, was fully rewarded, for they succeeded in proving their captured man guilty, he receiving a sentence of twelve years' penal servitude on the 2nd of December, 1902.

To express their sympathy for Mr. Tart and also to show the greatness of their pleasure upon his recovery, a great crowd of citizens gathered at the Town Hall on October 28th, 1902 and presented him with a handsome piece of plate and a cheque for three hundred guineas.

During Mr. Tart's disablement he was the recipient of sympathetic messages and inquiries from all classes in the community, amongst whom were the following:–

His Excellency Sir Harry Rawson, K.C.B.

Sir W. J. Lyne.

Rt. Hon. G. H. Reid, P.C.

Sir John See.

Hon. B. R. Wise, Attorney General.

Hon. John Kidd, Minister for Mines.

Members of the Federal and State Parliaments.

The Archbishop of Sydney.

Mr. Justice Simpson.

Mr. Justice Pring.

Mr. Justice Stephen, Acting Chief Justice.
Sir Geo. R. Dibbs.
Sir Wm. McMillan.
Bishop of Newcastle.
Bishop of Gippsland.
Moderator of the Presbyterian Assembly.
President of the Methodist Conference.
The Sisters of Charity.
Congregational, Baptist, and other denominations.
The Jewish Ministers.
The Officers of the Salvation Army.
Senator Nield.
Sydney Smith, M.H.R.
Joseph Cook, M.H.R.
Consuls of Foreign Nations.
Hon. Robert Fowler, M.L.C.
Hon. Edward Greville, M.L.C.
Hon. Alexander Kethel, M.L.C.
Hon. A. W. Meeks, M.L.C.
J. S. Hawthorne, Esq., M.L.A.
George Anderson, Esq., M.L.A.
John Hurley, Esq., M.L.A.
R. W. W. McCoy, Esq., M.L.A.
Thomas Jessep, Esq., M.L.A.
John Haynes, Esq., M.L.A.
W. M. Fehon, Esq., Railway Commissioner.
Medical and Legal Professions.
Representatives of the City, Suburban and Country Press.
Municipalities, Ashfield.
Charitable Institutions.
Numerous Societies, Masonic Lodges and Officers of the Military Forces.
Government Officers.
Inspector-General Fosbery.
Parliamentary Staff.
The Chinese Community.
Commercial and Shipping Community.
Sporting Clubs.
Tramway and Railway Employees.
Bandsmen, Cabmen, 'Busmen, Carters.
Members of Fire Brigades.
Members of Hospital Staffs.
Newsboys.
Factory Girls and Boys.
His own Employees and ex-Employees.
Old friends 70 and 80 years of age called personally.
Ashfield neighbours called daily, like a swarm of bees.

Some hundreds of letters, cards, and telegrams from Tasmania, Queensland, New Zealand and Victoria.

"Evening News," 2nd September, 1902.
MR. QUONG TART.

At the Hotel Australia on Monday, Senator Nield presided over a thoroughly representative meeting, which had been called to express abhorrence at the recent dastardly attack upon Mr. Quong Tart, and to express the deepest sympathy with Mr. Tart, and wish him a speedy recovery.

Mr. Hawthorne, M.L.A., moved: "That this meeting express its horror at the dastardly attempt made upon the life of Mr. Quong Tart, and deeply sympathises with him in his suffering, and wishes him a speedy recovery." Mr. Broughton, M.L.A., seconded the resolution, which was supported by gentlemen who have known Mr. Tart for over 30 years. The motion was carried unanimously. Mr. Justice G. B. Simpson then moved: "That this meeting desires that Mr Tart's worth as a citizen should be acknowledged in a substantial manner, and that a subscription list be opened for the purpose of presenting him with a purse of sovereigns, in recognition of his many generous and philanthropic actions." Mr. J. P. Wright seconded the motion, which also received a lot of support, and was carried unanimously.

Mr. W. R. G. Lee, one of the Chinese residents in Sydney present, said he desired to thank the meeting for the good feeling that existed. He said the actions of the people of Sydney only showed that any man, no matter what colour or nationality, could win the esteem of a British community, if by his life he showed that he deserved it. (Applause.)

Messrs. J. P. Wright and F. E. Winchcombe, M.L.A., were appointed hon. treasurers, and Messrs. Alderman Fitzgerald, A. J. Kelynack, and R. M. McC. Anderson, hon. secretaries. About £53 was subscribed in the room.

"Those who can appreciate public spirit, true benevolence, and the fervent desire (which has been attended by pronounced success) of a man of another race to identify himself with our life and our interests, will rejoice that definite steps have been taken to express to Quong Tart the hearty sympathy of the community in his recent trouble. Quong Tart, it will be remembered, was recently murderously attacked and robbed by a ruffian who gained admission to the injured gentleman's office. A representative meeting, held at the Australia Hotel yesterday, determined not only to show, but to express in practical form, sympathy with the victim. No less should or could be done, considering that Quong Tart has ever been among the foremost to lend a helping hand to any cause that needed assistance. The matter was taken up very warm-heartedly at the meeting, and it is hoped the result will prove that striking generosity can be fittingly acknowledged by Mr. Tart's fellow citizens."

"Star," 2nd September, 1902.

QUONG TART TESTIMONIAL.

At a Public Meeting, held at the Australia Hotel on Monday, it was resolved that a subscription list be opened for the purpose of presenting Mr. Quong Tart with a testimonial by way of showing public sympathy with him in connection with the recent murderous assault. Subscriptions towards this object are invited, and remittances may be sent to the Honourary Treasurers, namely,

Mr. J. P. WRIGHT, 280 Elizabeth Street.

Mr. F. E. WINCHCOMBE, 48 Bridge Street.

Or to the Honourary Secretaries,

J. D. FITZGERALD, Town Hall, Sydney.

ARTHUR KELYNACK, Denman Chambers.

R. M. M'C. ANDERSON, Pyrmont.

The Editor of the "Star" will receive any subscriptions forwarded to him.

Presentation to Mr. Quong Tart.

As Reported by "The Daily Telegraph"

Sydney, 17th October, 1902.

The vestibule of the Town Hall was crowded to overflowing last night, when Mr. Quong Tart was presented with a silver salver and a cheque for 300 guineas by the Mayor of Sydney (Mr. T. Hughes), on behalf of the citizens. Mr. Quong Tart was made the central figure of this demonstration on the occasion of his restoration to health after the recent assault upon him in his rooms, Queen Victoria Markets.

There were present, besides the Mayor:–Mr. G. H. Reid, Mr. Bennett (representing the State Government), Mr. Justice G. B. Simpson, Mr. J. H. Want, M.L.C., Mr. A. W. Meeks, M.L.C., Mr. Hogue, M.L.A., and several aldermen of the city.

The Mayor, who made the presentation on behalf of the citizens, referred to Mr. Quong Tart as one of the most public-spirited men in the city. (Applause.) He was associated, he said, with every good movement, and was free from prejudice; and he was glad to congratulate him, on behalf of the citizens, upon his recovery. (Cheers.)

Mr. Bennett first apologised for the unavoidable absence of Sir John See. Personally he said he admired Mr. Quong Tart as one of the most loyal and patriotic British citizens. (Cheers.) Mr. Tart had been forward in every good movement of citizenship (cheers), and he was glad to see such large numbers of ladies and gentlemen present to do him honour, and to sympathise with him in the recent event, which everybody was now aware of. (Cheers.) He was quite sure that both the citizens present and those who were not felt great sympathy with Mr. Tart in the most dastardly assault that was recently made upon him. (Loud applause.)

Mr. J. H. Want claimed that he was one of the oldest friends of Mr. Quong Tart. (Cheers.) Mr. Tart's career had always been characterised by good and splendid deeds. "I have known him," said Mr. Want, "since he was about as big as a bit of chalk — (laughter) — and upon my word, it is not a bad way to describe him, for wherever he goes he leaves a white mark behind him. (Laughter and loud cheers.) He was sure all the citizens felt sincerely glad that the attempt on his life failed, and that he was spared to live and continue his good works as a worthy citizen." (Cheers.)

Mr. A. W. Meeks, M.L.C., in the course of a few remarks, paid a high tribute to Mr. Quong Tart's popularity and personal good nature, and the prominent part he had always taken in philanthropic movements on behalf of his own countrymen and of Australians. (Cheers.)

Professor Anderson Stuart spoke in a similar strain.

Archdeacon Langley offered Mr. Quong Tart his congratulations upon the manifestation of the love and goodwill he had so worthily received from the people of Sydney.

Mr. J. P. Wright also expressed his pleasure at being able to take part in so magnificent a demonstration to Mr. Tart. (Cheers.)

Mr. Winchcombe, M.L.A., said he was glad to be able to say, as a member of the committee for managing this demonstration, that not only did subscriptions for the fund come unsolicited from remote parts of New South Wales, but from New Zealand — (cheers) — and the other States. (Cheers.)

Mr. W. R. G. Lee, one of Mr. Tart's countrymen, said he desired, on behalf of the Chinese citizens, not only to congratulate Mr. Tart upon the present expression of the citizens' good feeling, but to thank the people of Sydney and other places for the kindly manner in which they regarded their fellow citizen. (Cheers.) He was convinced that this demonstration would bear good fruit in the future. (Cheers.)

Mr. Quong Tart, who was received with vociferous applause, returned his sincere thanks for the presentation and the excellent demonstration in honour of his restoration to health. (Cheers.) Mr. Tart expressed his astonishment that he should ever be attacked. (Cheers.) He never attacked anybody. (Cheers.) Mr. Tart went on to refer to his friends, the Right Honourable George Reid — (cheers and laughter) — Mr. Justice G. B. Simpson — (cheers) — and Judge "Jack" Want. (Cheers and laughter.) He had received expressions of goodwill from residents of Victoria, South Australia, as well as other States, and the colony of New Zealand, as well as from His Excellency the Governor and "down to the Federal Government." (Boisterous laughter and cheers.) Mr. Tart said he was convinced that a man who did his duty honestly and fearlessly could always be assured of the good-will of his fellow citizens. (Cheers.)

Mr. George Reid, in moving a vote of thanks to the Mayor, claimed Mr. Tart as a fellow Scotsman. (Loud laughter.) Mr. Tart was the only man he knew who had the true Gaelic accent. (Laughter and cheers.) Mr. Reid proceeded to pay a high tribute to Mr. Tart's citizenship. No man in the community, he said, had lived a more honest, honourable, charitable, and Christian life than Mr. Tart had done. (Cheers.)

The Mayor, having acknowledged the vote of thanks, a most enthusiastic meeting closed.

Names of Contributors to the Quong Tart Testimonial.

J. P. WRIGHT

F. E. WINCHCOMBE

GEO. FISHBURN

D. J. MONK

E. JOHN FOX

M. J. COULON

DANIEL HOGAN

W. ALDENHOVEN

CHARLES VIDER

OLIVER WANSEY

J. J. HERLIHY

FARMER & SETTLER ASSOCIATION

A. L. PARKE

ROBT. FOWLER

ROBT. FOWLER, Junr.

W. E. SMITH

ALEX. KETHEL, M.L.C.

JAMES BROWN

ALFD. L. E. IRWIN

JOHN D. FITZGERALD

RICHARD TEECE

SUPERINTENDENT BRENNAN

R. J. LUKEY

F. W. WEBB, C.M.G.

E. C. V. BROUGHTON

GEO. NEWTON

ALLEN TAYLOR & CO.

EDWD. A. RENNIE

GEO. E. CRANE & SONS

RESCH'S WAVERLEY BREWERY

DAVID JONES & CO.

MRS. J. GRAHAME

J. C. MAYNARD

G. & C. HOSKINS

JOHNSON & VICARS

ALD. R. G. WATKINS

THOS. CORREY

H. M. NEALE

STOTT & HOARE

JOHN POMEROY

JOHN COLLINS

MRS. JOHN COLLINS

MRS. J. R. BRODIE

"DAILY TELEGRAPH" CO.

S. F. BLACKMORE

BURNS, PHILP, & CO.

HENRY L. NATHAN

DR. WM. CHISHOLM

JOHN MACPHERSON

JOHN MILLS, J.P.

F. BUCKLE

DUGALD THOMSON, M.H.R.

SAMUEL COOK

REV. JOSEPH BEST

JOHN McEVOY & SONS

WM. McINTYRE

CHAS. H. KERRY

A. S. MURRAY

STARKEY & STARKEY

JOHN SANDS

ASHFIELD BOROUGH BRASS BAND

"SALT"

DRS. BLACKWOOD & J. J. KELLY

H. BARTLETT

B. BYRNES

THOS. BLUNDELL

JAS. P. TREADGOLD

SENATOR J. T. WALKER

JAMES POWELL

HUGH DIXSON

GIBBS, BRIGHT & CO.

WRIGHT, HEATON, & CO.

SIR WILLIAM McMILLAN, K.C.M.G.

A. DARE & SON

A. W. S. GREGG

J. P. GRAY

MINTER, SIMPSON & CO.

A. R. MINTER

THOS. HENLEY

JUSTICE G. B. SIMPSON

JUSTICE STEPHEN

HARDIE & GORMAN

W. P. WELCH

JOHN YOUNG

JAMES MARKS

HON. W. J. TRICKETT

CRITCHETT WALKER, C.M.G.

HON. J. H. WANT, M.L.C.

ROBERT ANDERSON

JAMES ALDCORN

A. S. GORDON

GORDON & GOTCH

MRS. E. E. WATSON

PROF. ANDERSON STUART

A. J. RILEY

MASTER PLUMBERS AND SANITARY
ENGINEERS' ASSOCIATION.

W. G. JUDD

THE HOONG FOOK TONG SOCIETY

W. R. G. LEE

LOCK SHIN TONG

SUNG TACK TONG

WAN CHAN CHEW

HOR KONG

QUONG HING CHONG

SUN HING JAN

QUAN LEE

CHOW KUM

SUN JOHNSON

CHAS. DAT

WONG CHEW FOON

CHAN KWING FOO

NIE YEE

SOO HOO CHEONG

CHUN SHIN TONG

ONE YEE TONG

YEE HING

SEUNG KEE

JAN KWONG

MING LYE

FOO DART

MING JEUNG

CHAS. BOWN

JAMES JACKSON

W. H. McCLELLAND

W. R. GAINFORD

A. W. CLAPHAM

JOHN H. GOODLET

REV. W. WOOLLS RUTLEDGE

FREDERIC OVER

JAMES MILSON

REV. CANON VAUGHAN

TIY LOY

DART SHING

NIE MEN

YEW CHONG

CHAN MOY

TUY CHONG

SHANG WAR

CHEUCK SHING

LAM BO

BO SHAN

YEE LEE

HOCK TING

TSZE KEE

DUCK WHY

CHIP MUN

GAH TIPP

CHEUNG DEW

MING YEW

CHUNG HOW

MAN KEW

MING KUM

LUM WING

SHIN KWAI

YEE WING

BING YEM

LOUEY YUEY

NIE KWONG

HARRY J. LEE

JOHN ABLONG

WM. WONG GOLDTOWN

WING SANG & CO.

HIP WAR

HIP CHONG

W. SWANN

J. W. WITHERS

GEO. FISHBURN

THOS. BERGIN

S. H. YOUNG

T. F. BYRNE

J. BEST

W. LAING

SMITH & KING

JOHN S. ABRAHAM

F. ENGLEHERT

P. ROARTY

J. A. REID

GEO. BOWING

GEO. LIGGINS

C. W. BLAKENEY

W. R. PALMER

W. B. HARRIS

E. L. & CO.

JAS. GREEN

W. E. V. ROBSON

CHINA NAVIGATION CO.

R. T. REMINGTON

NIE TSZE	JOHN T. DUFF
MAN SUEY	QUING YOUNG & CO.
MING SOON	C. J. HENTY
NAM YEE	T. J. ALLISON
NEE WING	C. MORRISON
HIN KWONG	H. C. McCULLOCK
SHEE LIN	S. H. LAMBTON
POY CHEONG	EDWD. GREVILLE
GOON SEUNG	T. J. WEST
TSZE LEONG	JAMES PAUL
CHAN SHEUCK	— AVERY
MOY PING	— WARD
YAM QUOY	F. H. GREY
LOUEY PYE	G. H. WESTCOTT
DEW FOOK	JOSEPH MEDCALF
CHIN KWOON	SUN QUONG TONG
LOY FOO	CHONG LEE COFE
KEE SHIN	ARCHDEACON LANGLEY
MOY KYE	JAMES WING
NGA SHING	REV. GEE SOO HOO TEN
YEW FOON	ROBT. McKILLOP
MAN SOON	MOFFITT BURNS
HOONG WAY	J. S. HAWTHORNE
KWOK TSING	GEORGE TAYLOR
MING KEE	J. M. SMAIL
MOY CHAN FAT	ROBERT ADAM MACKINTOSH
LEE CHEE	EDWIN RICHARDS
C. B. PAYNE	F. G. IRVINGTON DEVINE
THE ARCHBISHOP OF SYDNEY.	E. LINDSAY THOMPSON
JOHN WALLACE	YIP CHUN MOON
MRS. SUN JOHNSON	NG TUK YUK
W. MORISON	NG TUNG CHE
W. H. SIMPSON	NG TUNG SHEW

CARL MUSSMAUN

C. H. G. TREMLETT

ALBERT E. CHAPMAN

S. H. HARRIS & CO.

CAPT. CRAIG

THOS. GLASSOP

T. H. NESBITT

W. G. LAYTON

R. R. DOUGAN

J. N. BREDEN

S. H. SOLOMON

W. M. GORDON

CAPT. MILLARD

JOHN DART

SENATOR J. C. NEILD

HUNTER McPHERSON

T. SINCLAIR

H. L. NUMN

A FRIEND

N. W. LOGAN

B. JAMES

S. BENT

W. R. G. LEE & FAMILY

E. WATTS

P. I. NELLIGAN

TOI LOONG KUN

CHEW FOOK JAW

LEE JAW

YAP CHOW PING

LAW YANG

YAP BOW MOW

YAP TOONG

MOY YOU WAI

CHEONG SHING KEE

WONG CHIN KING

NG KEN YEN

NG TIY OU

CHAU GHEONG SUN

CHAI LUM SHING

AH TAK

CHANG KIT TYE

CHANG FUNG WING

MACK YIK YUEN

SHAM YUT

SUN SUEY YUEN

NG PIN HOCK

LEW SHE WEI

NG TUNG HEM

JAS. AH CHUEY

YIP SHIN

YIP PAK NIN

NG HING PON

NG YEN WING

WONG KUM FOON

CHEONG YUEN HANG

NG YEN CHOY

YIP AH WAH

HAM JAW HIN

LOOK SHEW TONG

NG SIK KONG

LOUEY TZE LOY

YEE LIN TZE

HUI WAH CHUCK

NG CHEONG

NG TIY SHING

HIN LOCK

AH CHOOK	GO BO BROS.
JEANG HIN TSANG	F. R. WATSON
W. M. FEHON, COMMISSIONER FOR RAILWAYS	J. H. G. GEO. MUSGROVE
JAMES WARD	JAMES W. ABIGAIL
SIR JOHN SEE, PREMIER	THOS. HUGHES (MAYOR)
HON. L. F. HEYDON, LEGISLATIVE COUNCIL	A. J. KELYNACK
	W. F. McMANEMY
CAPT. A. W. WEBBER	A. H. NEWMAN
JOHN WILLIAMSON & SONS	MARK J. HAMMOND

Copy of Resolution and Prayer.

On the afternoon of the 19th October, notwithstanding the inclement weather, a large number of members of Lodge Tranquility, No. 42 Sydney, waited on Bro. Quong Tart at his residence, Ashfield, and the Wor. Master (Wor. Bro. M. G. Costa), on behalf of his brethren, presented him with an illuminated copy of the resolution and prayer, emphasising the tribute to be from members of the Craft personally, and not as a corporate body of citizens.

Thanksgiving to the Great Architect of The Universe for the recovery of our Brother Quong Tart.

THE LODGE OF TRANQUILITY, No. 42, N.S.W.

Wor. Bro. MOSS COSTA, W.M.

At the Regular Monthly Meeting, held on 11th September, 1902, the Worshipful Master, Wor. Bro. Moss Costa, said:—

Brethren: It has pleased Almighty God to stay the hand of assault in the recent attack on our Brother, QUONG TART. But for the merciful intervention of the G.A., our Brother might now have been removed from us. However, in His excellent mercy, He, Who is all merciful, has spared our Brother to us, and has restored him again to health and strength. We render Him all gratitude, and I call upon Wor. Bro Chaplain to acknowledge in prayer our hearty thanksgiving.

The Chaplain, Wor. Bro. J. Herman, offered the following prayer:

We render Thee all praise, O Giver of all mercies, for the protection Thou has recently afforded to our Brother, QUONG TART. Thou hast, in Thy goodness, stayed the hand of the violent, and hast brought again to health and strength our Brother whom we love. We pray for Thine unfortunate creature, who, for the sake of a little gain, might, but for Thy prevention, have been a murderer. Show him, O merciful Lord, the error of his ways, and forgive him his sin. And accept our thanks for Thy mercy to our Brother. May he in Thy goodness be long spared to work with and for us, that we may enjoy his companionship, and that in him our Noble Art may be exemplified, so that the world may be made brighter and better by his presence. Grant him, O merciful Lord, the full grace of all Masonic Virtues, and make him a living pattern of that strong Faith, lively Hope and all abiding Charity, which, we trust, will in due time entitle him to be numbered in the Grand Lodge above.

So mote it be.

Sydney, 11th September, 1902.

Apologies were announced for non-attendance from several members of the Lodge. Wor. Bro. Herman, Wor. Bro. Maerker, Wor. Bro. F. Smith, the Senior Warden (Bro. Hogbin), and the Secretary (V. Wor. Bro. Bretnall) spoke in appreciation of the recipient.

Bro. Noel (Organist) sang a sacred solo. Bro. Quong Tart responded, and spoke of the gratification of his family and self at the mark of esteem the memento represented. He well remembered the impressive ceremony of his initiation by Wor. Bro. Bretnall, and the action that day exemplified the bond of fellowship which existed.

Subsequently the visitors were entertained at refreshment. Wor. Bro. Costa presided. A toast list was gone through, which evinced the personal feelings of regard in which the host and his family were held.

Death and Funeral.

Quong Tart is dead. Such was the sad news whispered across the wires of the State on the 27th of July, 1903. By a life of integrity, unselfishness, and self-sacrificing toil, he won the esteem of everyone — his name being a household word throughout the whole land, and news of his death came as a great shock to all.

His illness was brief, lasting only a week. On Monday, suffering from the effects of a chill, he went to bed. Dr. Traill, of Burwood, his medical attendant, was summoned, and found that pleurisy existed, but he was not considered to be in danger. As the week wore on he took a decided turn for the worse, and at nine o'clock on Sunday night he passed away, death being due to failure of the heart's action. He was only fifty-three years of age.

As a citizen he took an active part in everything which was for the advancement of the country; as a philanthropist he gave lavishly of his abundance to all objects and institutions worthy of assistance; as a Christian he kept his life unsullied.

His life was instinct with the highest ideals, the Brotherhood of Man and the Fatherhood of God. In his belief in these he never wavered.

Thus, thinking of his fellows and whispering softly, "Abide with Me; fast falls the eventide," the flood gates of the West gently closed and shut his life forever from our view.

The funeral took place two days later, the remains being interred in the Church of England section of the Necropolis, in the presence of a large attendance of all sections of the community, thus testifying to the esteem and respect in which he was held. An immense concourse of people assembled in the immediate vicinity of his late residence, "Gallop House," Arthur Street, Ashfield, while the streets, through which the cortege passed on its way to the local railway station, were lined with spectators.

The approaches to the station were also thronged with people, the male portion of whom reverently uncovered their heads as the coffin was being carried from the hearse to the special train, which conveyed the funeral party to Rookwood.

The coffin in which the body, fully dressed in the costume of a Mandarin, was placed, was of lead, encased in a handsome casket of polished oak, with silver mountings, and bore the inscription —

QUONG TART.

Died 26th of July, 1903,

Aged 53 Years.

At Rest.

And on the lid was placed his Masonic Apron.

A brief service was held in the drawing-room by the Rev. Joseph Best, of St. James' Church, Croydon, and at 2.30 the cortage left "Gallop House" in the following order:–

The Professional Musicians Association Brass Band (specially engaged by the Lin Yik Tong Chinese Benevolent Society); about two hundred of his fellow countrymen; the hearse, drawn by four horses, containing the coffin; the carriage containing the floral emblems; the relatives of the deceased; the representatives of social and public bodies, and the general mourners.

As the cortage moved away, the band commenced Chopin's beautiful composition, "March Funebre," which was continued until the railway station was reached.

Numbers of people proceeded by special and ordinary train to the Necropolis, Rookwood, and to the number of about fifteen hundred marched in procession to the grave, where Archdeacon Langley, assisted by the Revs. Joseph Best and Soo Hoo Ten read the burial service.

The Rev. Soo Hoo Ten read a portion of the service in Chinese, the Archdeacon delivered a brief and impressive address, and the Very Wor. Bro. F. R. Bretnall, Past Grand Registrar and Secretary of the Lodge Tranquility, to which Mr. Tart belonged, read the Masonic burial service, while about forty of the brethren of the Order stood round the grave in regalia, and at the close of the service paid the last token of respect by placing the sprigs of acacia on the coffin. The devotional proceedings were concluded with the singing of Mr. Tart's favourite hymn, "Abide with Me."

Many hundreds of beautifully worded letters and telegrams of sympathy were received by the widow, amongst them being one from the State Governor, the late Sir Harry Rawson, and others from Sir William Lyne, Sir Edmund Barton (the Federal Premier), the Railway Commissioners, Mr. Justice Simpson, the Mayor and Aldermen of Ashfield, and old friends of Mr. Tart's.

The chief Chinese merchants of the city closed their premises as a mark of respect, and the flag of the Ashfield Town Hall was flown half-mast.

His funeral was one of the largest ever seen in Sydney. Many came by special and other trains; great multitudes lined the streets and blocked the railway station. A great number of floral tributes were sent to lie upon the grave. The press spoke of him in feeling and commendatory terms.

The Sydney "Daily Telegraph" — "Few names were better known locally or more highly esteemed than that of deceased."

The "Sydney Morning Herald" — "Mr. Tart was in the best sense of the word a good citizen. His assistance was always forthcoming for a good cause. Between the Chinese citizens and the general community he stood as a kind of connecting link, highly respected by both."

The "Town and Country Journal" — "No more genuine or widespread regret probably would be occasioned by the news of the death of any citizen than will be caused by the announcement that Mr. Quong Tart, the popular Chinese merchant of Sydney, has joined the Great Majority. In losing Mr. Tart, Sydney has lost a citizen who has always acted up to citizenship in the highest sense of the word."

Extract from "Evening News," 5th August, 1903.

Mrs. Quong Tart has received messages from all parts of Australia, conveying the sympathy of the many friends of her late husband. The messages, which include letters and telegrams from all classes of the community, are so numerous that Mrs. Tart is unable to reply to them all except by a general message through the Press, and she has, therefore, requested the "Evening News" to express her grateful acknowledgment for those condolences, and for the many floral tributes which were also sent.

Return Thanks.

Mrs. Quong Tart, of "Gallop House," Ashfield, desires to express her thanks for the many letters and telegrams of sympathy and floral tributes she has received on the death of her husband. Mr. Tart had so many friends in all parts of Australasia, and their generous messages of condolence have been so numerous that Mrs. Tart is unable to reply to them individually, and she hopes, therefore, that they will accept this as a grateful acknowledgment of their kind messages.

This man's life and works recall Longfellow's memorable lines in the soul soothing and yet inspiring "Psalm of Life" —

> Lives of great men all remind us
> We can make our lives sublime,
> And, departing, leave behind us
> Footprints on the sands of time —
> Footprints that perhaps another,
> Sailing o'er life's solemn main,
> A forlorn and shipwrecked brother,
> Seeing, shall take heart again."

IN MEMORIAM.

> Alas, poor Quong! A man of sterling worth,
> Though not of our nationality — proud of Chinese birth.
> Honoured by his countrymen, and by his nation, too —
> Mandarin of Crystal Button — respected, loved and true.
> Erect a noble monument to make a noble fame,
> To all alike, both rich and poor, he ever was the same.
> God rest him and reward him with an everlasting name.

C. E. WILTON.

Sydney, 27th July, 1903.

The few words on his monument erected by his wife, read — "A true husband, father, and friend. — Greatly missed."

THE LIFE OF QUONG TART:

OR,

HOW A FOREIGNER SUCCEEDED IN A BRITISH COMMUNITY.

Compiled and Edited by:

MRS. QUONG TART.

ILLUSTRATED.

PRICE   -   -   3/-

(Copyright)

Printed and Published by
W. M. MACLARDY, "BEN FRANKLIN" PRINTING WORKS.
SYDNEY, 1911.

Yours truly
Margaret W. Tart

Yours truly

Quong Tart

QUONG TART AT HOME.

QUONG TART AT HOME.

QUONG TART—MANDARIN.

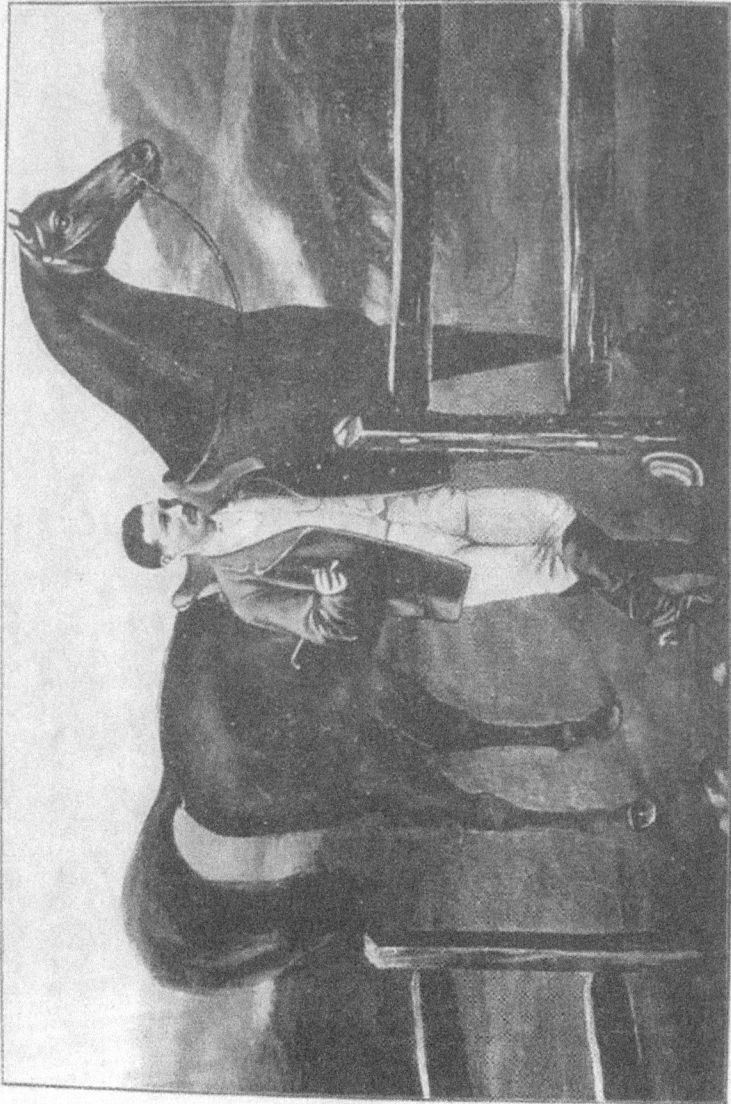

QUONG TART—A HORSEMAN, and NOBBY His Horse, for years in Braidwood.

DIRECTORS OF THE CHINESE BENEVOLENT SOCIETY IN 1902.

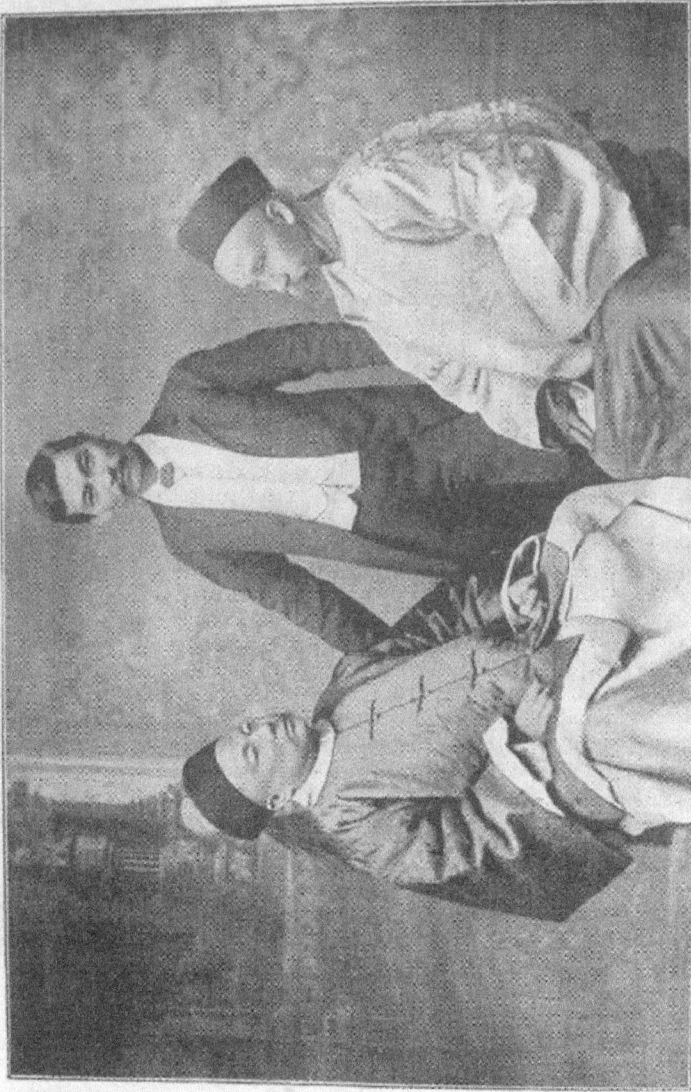

CHINESE AMBASSADORS (The First Men of Rank sent by His Imperial Majesty to visit Australia

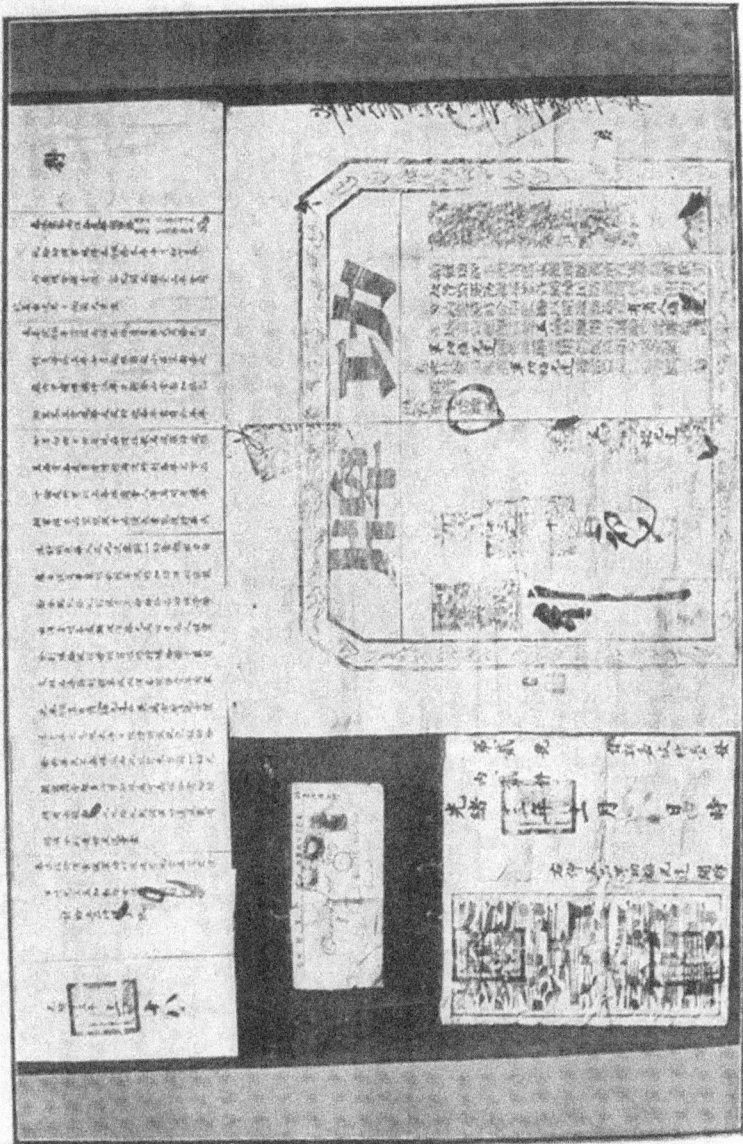

HONOR CONFERRED UPON QUONG TART BY HIS
IMPERIAL MAJESTY.

QUONG TART, MANDARIN, AND MRS. TART IN COSTUME.

QUONG TARTAN
OR
HE WOULD BE A SCOTS-MAN.

TELEGRAM FROM BATHURST.   28th January, 1902.

QUONG TART, Queen Victoria Markets, Sydney.

Cheers for Quong Tart and Health with musical honors at Bathurst
Highland Gathering last night.—DONALD THAIN, President.

101

QUONG TART—A MILITARY OFFICER.

FAMILY GROUP.

GEORGE HENRY BRUCE TART.

(The infant at the time of Quong Tart's death, not included in the Group).

QUONG TART, League of Wheelman Starter, with
MR. BAGNALL.

QUONG TART—A CRICKETER.

CITIZENS' PRESENTATION SALVER.

THE LATE MR. QUONG TART.—THE FUNERAL CORTEGE LEAVING THE DECEASED'S RESIDENCE AT ASHFIELD.

FUNERAL OF THE LATE QUONG TART, ASHFIELD, JULY 28, 1903.

Procession of 200 Chinese, Headed by a Band from the Professional Musicians' Association.

THE HEARSE.

WREATHS.

www.ingramcontent.com/pod-product-compliance
Lightning Source LLC
LaVergne TN
LVHW052341080426
835508LV00045B/3183